Statistics for Economics

Statistics for Economics

Shahdad Naghshpour

Statistics for Economics

First published in 2012 by
Business Expert Press, LLC
222 East 46th Street, New York, NY 10017
www.businessexpertpress.com

ISBN-13: 978-1-60649-403-5 (paperback)

ISBN-13: 978-1-60649-404-2 (e-book)

DOI 10.4128/9781606494042

Business Expert Press Economics collection

Collection ISSN: 2163-761X (print)
Collection ISSN: 2163-7628 (electronic)

Cover design by Jonathan Pennell
Interior design by Exeter Premedia Services Private Ltd.,
Chennai, India

First edition: 2012

10 9 8 7 6 5 4 3 2 1

Printed in the United States of America.

To Donna
SN

Abstract

Statistics is the branch of mathematics that deals with real-life problems. As such, it is an essential tool for economists. Unfortunately, the way the concept of statistics is introduced to students is not compatible with the way economists think and learn. The problem is worsened by the use of mathematical jargon and complex derivations. However, as this book demonstrates, neither is necessary. This book is written in simple English with minimal use of symbols, mostly for the sake of brevity and to make reading literature more meaningful.

All the examples and exercises in this book are constructed within the field of economics, thus eliminating the difficulty of learning statistics with examples from fields that have no relation to business, politics, or policy. Statistics is, in fact, not more difficult than economics. Anyone who can comprehend economics can understand and use statistics successfully within this field.

In my opinion, the most important aspect of statistics is its ability to summarize the information embedded in numerous data into few parameters and to capture the essence of data. The ability to capture the inherent core meaning of data from seemingly random and varying bits of information is unique to statistics. It seems that somehow statistics is able to find order in chaos.

This book utilizes Microsoft Excel to obtain statistical results, as well as to perform additional necessary computations. Microsoft Excel is not the software of choice for performing sophisticated statistical analysis. However, it is widely available, and almost everyone has some degree of familiarity with it. Using Excel will eliminate the need for students and readers to buy and learn new software, the need that itself would prove to be another impediment to learning and using statistics.

Keywords

null and alternative hypotheses, standardization, normal distribution function, statistical inference, test statistics, t distribution function, F distribution function, parameter, mean, standard deviation, interpretation and analysis, coefficient of determination, degrees of freedom, sampling distribution of sample statistics, standard error, unbiased, consistent, efficient, central limit theorem, margin of error, individual error, average error, mean squared error, analysis of variance (ANOVA)

Contents

Contents

Statistics Is the Science of Finding Order in Chaos

I wrote this manuscript to share my affection for statistics and to show that comprehending statistics does not require mastery of mathematical jargon or complex formulations and derivation. I do not claim that upon learning the material in this book you will be considered a statistician or can start a career in statistics; however, I promise you will have a much better understanding of the subject and will be able to apply its methods in the areas to which they apply. I also hope you will gain the wisdom of knowing where the things you have learned will not work and realize that you have to learn new material to handle such cases.

Statistics is the science of life. It does not live outside of real life. Conclusions in statistics are probabilistic in nature as compared to deterministic in most branches of mathematics. Every aspect of life benefits from statistics.

Learning statistics is like learning to play an instrument or learning a foreign language. Simply reading and comprehending the material is not sufficient; you also need to practice, and memorizing the material is also important. It is not sufficient to know the material or where to find it. The same is true about learning foreign languages. Unless you would like to walk around with a dictionary or a statistics book under your arm, you must know the material by heart.

I am indebted to my wife Donna who has helped me in more ways than imaginable. I do not think I can thank her enough. I would like to thank Michael Webb and Candice Bright for their relentless assistance in all aspects of this book. He has been my most reliable source and I could always count on him. I also want to thank my graduate assistants Issam Abu-Ghallous and Brian Carriere. They have provided many hours of help with all aspects of the process. Without the help of Mike, Issam, and Brian, this book would not have been completed. I also would like to thank Madeline Gillette, Anthony Calandrillo, and Matt Orzechowski who read parts of the manuscript.

Introduction

Economics is a very interesting subject. The scope of the economic domain is vast. Economics deals with market structure, consumer behavior, investment, growth, fiscal policy, monetary policy, the roles of the bank, and so forth. The list can go on for quite some time. It also predicts how economic agents behave in response to changes in economic and noneconomic factors such as price, income, political party, stability, and so on. Economic theory, however, is not specific. For example, the theory proves that when the price of a good increases, the quantity supplied increases, provided all the other pertinent factors remain constant, which is also known as **ceteris paribus**. What the theory does not and cannot state is how much the quantity increases for a given increase in price. The answer to this question seems to be more interesting to most people than the fact that quantity will increase as a result of an increase in price. The truth is that the theory that explains the above relationship is important for economists. For the rest of the population, knowledge of that relationship is worthless if the magnitude is unknown. Assume for a 10% increase in price, the quantity increases by 1%. This has many different consequences if the quantity increases by 10%, and totally different consequences if the quantity increases by 20%. The knowledge of the magnitude of change is as important, if not more important, than the knowledge of the direction of change. In other words, predictions are valuable when they are specific.

Statistics is the science that can answer specific issues raised above. The science of statistics provides necessary theories that can provide the foundation for answering such specific questions. Statistics theory indicates the necessary conditions to set up the study and collect data. It provides the means to analyze and clarify the meaning of the findings. It also provides the foundation to explain the meaning of the findings using statistical inference.

In order to make an economic decision, it is necessary to know the economic conditions. This is true for all economic agents, from the smallest to the largest. The smallest economic agent might be an individual with little earning and disposable income, while the largest can be a multinational corporation with thousands of employees, or government. Briefly, we will discuss some of the main needs and uses of statistics in economics, and then present some uses of regression analysis in economics.

The first step in making any economic decision is to gain knowledge of the state of the economy. Economic condition is always in a state of flux. Sometimes it seems that we are not very concerned with mundane economic basics. For example, we may not try to forecast what the price of a loaf of bread is or a pound of meat. We know the average prices for these items; we consume them on a regular basis and will continue doing so as long as nothing drastic happens. However, if you were to buy a new car you would most likely call around and check some showrooms to learn about available features and prices because we tend not to have up to date information on big-ticket items or goods and services that we do not purchase regularly. The process described previously is a kind of sampling, and the information that you obtain is called **sample statistics**, which are used to make an informed decision about the average price of an automobile. When the process is performed according to strict and formal statistical methods, it is called **statistical inference**. The specific sample statistics is called sample mean. The **mean** is one of numerous statistical measures at the disposal of modern economists.

Another useful measure is the median. The **median** is a value that divides observations into two equal halves, one with values less than the median and the other with values more than median. Statistics explains when each measure should be used and what determines which one is the appropriate measure. Median is the appropriate measure when dealing with home prices or income. Applications of statistical analysis in economics are vast and sometimes reach to other disciplines that need economics for assistance. For example, when we need to build a bridge to meet economic, social, and even cultural needs of a community, it is important to find a reliable estimate of the necessary capacity of the bridge. Statistics indicates the appropriate measure to be used by teaching us whether we should use the median or the mode. It also provides insight on the role that variance plays in this problem. In addition to identifying the appropriate tools for the task at hand, statistics also provides the methods of obtaining suitable data and procedure for performing analysis to deliver the necessary inference.

One cannot imagine an economic problem that does not depend on statistical analysis. Every year, the Government Printing Office compiles the Economic Report for the President. The majority of the statistics in the report are fact-based information about different aspects of economics, however, many of the statistics are based on some statistical analysis, albeit descriptive statistics. **Descriptive statistics** provide simple, yet powerful insight to economic agents and enable them to make more informed decisions.

Another component of statistical analysis is inferential statistics. **Inferential statistics** allows the economist and political leaders to test hypotheses about economic conditions. For example, in the presence of inflation, the Federal Reserve Board of Governors may choose to reduce money supply to cool down the economy and slow down the pace of inflation. The knowledge of how much to reduce the supply of money is not only based on economic theory, but also depends on proper estimation of the final outcome.

Another widely used application of statistical analysis is in policy decision. We hear a lot about the erosion of the middle class or that the middle class pays a larger percentage of its income in taxes than do lower and upper classes. How do we know who the middle class is? A set dollar amount of income would be inadequate because of inflation although, we must admit, even a single dollar amount must also be obtained using statistics. However, statistical analysis has a much more meaningful and more elegant solution. The concept of interquartile range identifies the middle 50% of the population or income. Interquartile range was not designed to identify the middle 50%, and it is not explained in these terms; nevertheless, the combination of economics and statistics is used to identify the middle 50% for economics and policy decision purposes.

Knowledge of statistics can also help identify and comprehend daily news events. Recently, a report indicated that the chance of accident for teenage drivers increases by 40% when there are passengers in the car who are under 21 years of age. This is a meaningless report. Few teenagers drive alone or have passengers over 21 years of age. Total miles driven by teenagers when there are passengers less than 21 years of age far exceeds any other types of teenage driving. Other things equal, the more you drive, the higher the probability of an accident. This example indicates that knowledge of statistics is helpful in understanding everyday events and in making sound analyses.

One of the most important aspects of statistics is the discovery of rules that allow the use of a sample to draw inferences about population parameters. Inferential statistics allows us to make decisions about the possibility of an outcome based on its probability, not dissimilar to what we do in real life anyway. Life experience is private and is based on an individual. A friend is usually late, and based on that, we estimate his approximate arrival time. In statistics the process is formal. We take random samples, and based on statistical theories of sampling distribution and the probabilities of outcomes, we make inferences and predictions about the outcomes. In essence, statistics formalizes the human experience of estimation and makes predictions more formal and provides theoretical proofs for anticipated outcomes.

This book focuses on a few introductory topics in statistics and provides examples from economics. It takes a different orientation for covering the material than most other books. Chapters 1 and 2 cover descriptive statistics from tabular, graphical, and numeric points of view. A summary table of all the tools introduced in these chapters is provided in Chapter 1 to help you see the big picture of what belongs where. This grouping helps relate topics to each other. Chapter 3 provides some applications of these basic tools in different areas of economics. The purpose of Chapter 3 is to demonstrate that even simple statistics, when used properly, can be very useful and beneficial. Interestingly, some, if not most, of descriptive statistics are either intuitive or commonly utilized in everyday life. However, as the first three chapters reveal, it is useful to demonstrate their power using examples from economics.

Chapter 4 introduces some commonly used distribution functions. These will most likely be new for you. These distribution functions are used as yardsticks to measure different statistics to determine if they behave as expected, or they should be considered unusual outcomes. Interestingly, when we sample, the resulting sample statistics such as sample mean, follow certain distribution functions. These important properties are discussed in Chapter 5, titled Sampling Distribution of

Sample Statistics. Chapter 6 formally discusses estimation. Point estimation uses sample statistics directly, while confidence interval provides a range that covers population parameter with a desired level of confidence. Finally, Chapter 7 combines materials from Chapters 4 through 6 to perform statistical inference. Statistical inference is a probabilistic statement about the expected outcome of a study.

A volume like the present work is not sufficient to do justice to the subject. Every aspect of science is touched by statistics, to some extent. Therefore, specialty books about applications of statistics in different fields abound.

CHAPTER 1

Descriptive Statistics

Introduction

A simple fact of life is that most phenomena have a random component. Human beings have a natural height that is different than the natural height of a dog or a tree. However, human beings are not all of the same height. The usually small range is governed by random error. For example, the range of adult human height is roughly 52–75 inches. This does not mean that 100% of all mankind are in this range. The small portions that are outside this range are considered outliers. Summarizing the height of human beings is very common in statistics. However, in science, it is helpful to provide the associated level of confidence in a statement. For example, it is important to state that a particular percentage, say 90%, of human beings have a height between 58 and 72 inches. One might think that it is important, or may be even necessary, to provide a range that covers all cases. However, such a range may prove to be too wide to be of actual use. For example, one might be able to say with 100% certainty that the annual income in the United States is between $0 and $100,000,000,000. Although, the lower end is a certainty, the upper end need not be as definite. Granted that the chance of anyone making $100,000,000,000 in a year is very low, nevertheless, there is no compelling reason against it. Therefore, one has to provide the probability of someone making such a huge income. Since this chance is low, it would be more meaningful to state an income range for a meaningful majority, such as income range of 95% of people. It is more useful to know that 99% of all people in the United States earned less than $380,354 per individual return in 2008,[1] which is the same as saying that the top 1% made at least that much per individual return in the same year. According to the same source, the top 10% made more than $113,799 per individual return.

The actual percentage is not important and depends on the task at hand. For example, the government might want to help the middle class, which has been losing ground in economic terms, by granting them a tax break to lower their tax burden to a burden equivalent to that of the upper and lower classes. One way of determining the middle class income of a population is to find 50% of the people whose incomes are in the middle. Alternatively, this means to identify the cutoff income level for the lower 25% of incomes, and the cutoff income level for the upper 25% of incomes. The two cutoff incomes mark the income range that contains 50% of the incomes. Computations necessary to determine these and other useful values are the subject of **descriptive statistics**.

Descriptive statistics provides quick and representative information about a population or a sample. A typical man is 5′10″, the average temperature on July 4 is 89°, Olympic runners finish the 100 meter dash in under 10 seconds, the most common shoe size for women is seven, and so forth. These statistics are describing something of interest about the population and condense all the facts in a single parameter. Descriptive statistics is the science of summarizing and condensing information in few parameters.

There are many ways of condensing information to create descriptive statistics. Different types of data require different tools. Data can be **qualitative** or **quantitative**. These naming conventions actually refer to the way **variables** are measured and not the inherent characteristic of a phenomenon. In my opinion, these naming conventions are inaccurate. Variables are used for statistical analysis and are measured based on their characteristics. Sometimes, qualitative variables are called **categorical** variables. There are numerous **measurement scales**. Therefore, we focus on qualitative and quantitative variables.

In many cases, analyzing qualitative and quantitative variables requires different tools, but in some cases the tools are similar, if not identical, for both. However, the interpretations of qualitative and quantitative variables are usually different. Note that a population is not defined as either qualitative or quantitative. Rather, it is the variable of interest in the population that is either qualitative or quantitative. For example, the population can be defined as a person. If the age of the person is of interest, then the variable is quantitative; but if the gender of the person is of interest, then the variable is qualitative. If the population is a firm and the variable is pollution (the firm pollutes or does not pollute), then it is a qualitative variable. However, if the amount of pollution is of interest, then it is a quantitative variable.

Definition 1.1

Qualitative variables are non-numeric. They represent a label for a category of similar items. For example, the color of socks of students in a class is a qualitative data.

Definition 1.2

Quantitative variables are numerical and countable values. The distance each student has to travel to get to school is a quantitative data.

Measurement Scales

Variables must be measured in a meaningful way. The following is a brief description of different types of measurement scales. Over time, different vocabularies and naming conventions have evolved in naming different measurement scales. It is not possible to decipher an appropriate measurement scale by observing the measurement. Instead, the method of measurement and the quantities that are measured must be examined to determine the extent of the meaning one can assign to the numeric values, and hence, identify the measurement scale. Most of the methods in this text require an interval or measurement scales with stronger relational requirements.

Definition 1.3

Nominal or *categorical* data are the "count" of the number of times an event occurs. As an example for categorical data, countries might be grouped according to their policy toward trade and might be classified as open or closed economies. Care must be taken to assure that each case belongs to only one group. An ID number is an example of nominal data. As the relative size does not matter for nominal data, the customary arithmetic computations and statistical methods do not apply to these numbers.

Definition 1.4

When there are only two nominal types, the data is *dichotomous*. Dichotomous variables are also known as **dummy variables** in **econometrics**. When there is no particular order the dichotomous variable is called the **discrete dichotomous variable**. Gender is an example of a discrete dichotomous variable. When one can place an order on the type of data, as in the case of young and old, then the variable is a **continuous dichotomous variable.**

Definition 1.5

An *ordinal scale* indicates that data is ordered in some way. Although orders or ranks are represented by numerical values, such values are void of content and cannot be used for typical computations such as averages. The distances between ranks are meaningless. The income of the person who is ranked 20th in a group of ordered income is not twice the income of someone who is ranked 40th. In the ordinal scale only the comparisons "greater," "equal," or "less" are meaningful. This is a very important scale in economics, as in the case of utility and indifference curves. It is not necessary to measure the amount of utility one receives from different goods and services; it is sufficient to rank the utilities. The customary arithmetic computations and statistical methods do not apply to ordinal numbers.

Definition 1.6

A **Likert scale** is a special kind of ordinal scale where the subjects provide the ranking of each variable. Customarily, the numbers of the choices for ranking are odd numbers to allow the center value to represent the "neutral" case.

Definition 1.7

In an **interval scale**, the relative distances between any two sequential values are the same. In the interval scale, size of the difference between measurements is also important. Each numerical scale is actually measured from "accepted zero." This makes use of the type of scale irrelevant as in the case of Celsius and Fahrenheit scales for temperatures. Both scales have an arbitrary zero. Some arithmetic computations such as addition and subtraction are meaningful.

Definition 1.8

The *ratio scale* provides meaningful use of the ratio of measurements in addition to interval size and order of scales. For example, the ratio of sales, gross domestic product (GDP), and output are expressed as ratio scale.

There are numerous other measurement scales, but these have little practical use in economics. A classical work on measurement is by S. S. Stevens.[2]

Types of Available Tools

Descriptive statistics provides summaries of information about a population or sample, both of which will be defined shortly. The amount of information available is vast and comprehending their intrinsic value is difficult. Descriptive statistics provides some means of condensing massive amounts of information in as few **parameters** as possible.

Definition 1.9

A *parameter* is a characteristic of a population that is of interest. Parameters are constant and usually unknown.

Examples of parameters include population mean, population variance, and regression coefficients. One of the main purposes of statistics is to obtain information from a sample that can be used to make inferences about population parameters. The estimated value obtained from a sample is called a **statistic**.

Table 1.1. **Descriptive Statistics**

Qualitative Variables	Tabular Methods	Frequency		
		Relative Frequency		
	Graphical Methods	Bar Graphs		
		Pie Charts		
Quantitative Variables	Tabular Methods	Frequency Distribution		
		Relative Frequency		
		Cumulative Distribution		
		Percentiles		
		Quartiles		
		Hinges		
	Graphical Methods	Histograms		
		Ogive		
		Stem-and-Leaf		
		Dot Plot		
		Scatter Plot		
		Box Plot		
	Numerical Methods	Measures of Location	Mean	Ungrouped Data
				Grouped Data
			Trimmed Mean	
			Median	
			Mode	
		Measures of Dispersion	Range	
			Interquartile Range	
			Variance	Ungrouped Data
				Grouped Data
			Standard Deviation	
			Coefficient of Variation	
		Measures of Association	Covariance	
			Correlation Coefficient	

Table 1.1 summarizes the descriptive methods for quantitative and qualitative variables. Note that these are only the descriptive statistics and by no means all the methods at our disposal.

Definition 1.10

When data are summarized or organized to provide a better and more compact picture of reality, then data are *grouped*. The grouping can be in the form of relative frequency or summarized in cross tabulation tables or into classes.

Descriptive Statistics for Qualitative Variables

The available descriptive statistics for qualitative variables can be divided into **graphical** and **tabular** methods. Each one consists of several customarily used tools. In order to be able to graph the data, it must be tabulated in some fashion; therefore, we will discuss the tabular methods first.

Tabular Methods for Qualitative Variables

The most common tabular methods for qualitative variables are frequency and relative frequency.

Frequency Distribution for Qualitative Variables

A frequency distribution shows the frequency of occurrence for non-overlapping classes.

Example 1.1

In a small town a small company is responsible for refilling soda dispensers of 30 businesses. The type of business, the average number of cans of soda (in 100 cans), the gender of the business owner, and the race of business owner are presented in Table 1.2. Find the frequencies of the business types where soda dispensers are located.

(*Continued*)

8   STATISTICS FOR ECONOMICS

(*Continued*)

Table 1.2. *Some Information About Soda Dispensers*

Store type	Average	Gender	Race
Gas Station	3.8	Male	Black
Gas Station	3.5	Female	Black
Gas Station	2.6	Male	White
Mechanic Shop	2.1	Male	Black
Mechanic Shop	1.9	Male	White
Mechanic Shop	3.4	Female	White
Mechanic Shop	2.7	Male	White
Mechanic Shop	1.8	Female	Black
Mechanic Shop	3.7	Male	White
Mechanic Shop	4	Female	White
Mechanic Shop	1.9	Female	White
Mechanic Shop	2.6	Female	White
Drug Store	2.7	Female	White
Drug Store	2.4	Male	Black
Drug Store	3.6	Female	Black
Drug Store	3.2	Female	White
Drug Store	2.7	Male	White
Hardware Store	3.5	Male	Black
Hardware Store	1.8	Female	White
Hardware Store	3.4	Male	White
Hardware Store	2.8	Male	Black
Hardware Store	2.1	Female	White
Hardware Store	3.1	Female	White
Hardware Store	2.6	Male	White
Sporting Goods	1.7	Male	White
Sporting Goods	4	Female	White
Sporting Goods	3.2	Male	White
Sporting Goods	2.4	Female	Black
School	3.7	Female	White
Tire Shop	2.8	Female	White

(*Continued*)

Solution

A frequency distribution for the business type will clarify the information.

Gas Stations	ЖН	
Mechanic Shop	ЖН	////
Drug Store	////	
Hardware Store	ЖН	//
Sporting Goods	////	
School	/	
Tire Shop	/	

This certainly is an improvement, but Table 1.3 makes it even clearer and more condensed.

Table 1.3. Business Types, Frequencies, and Relative Frequencies of Locations

Location	Frequency
Gas Stations	3
Mechanic Shop	9
Drug Store	5
Hardware Store	7
Sporting Goods	4
School	1
Tire Shop	1
Total	30

It is easier to determine the locations, how many times each is restocked, as well as finding the most frequent, and the least frequent locations.

A table with 30 cells has been reduced to a two-column table with seven rows. If there were 20,000 locations and the types of business remained similar, the resulting table would not be any larger. While no one can really understand anything from a table with 20,000 entries, the resulting table would be very clear. This signifies the power of statistics to condense information in as few parameters as possible. The result can be graphed for more visual presentation. One possible graph is called a bar graph. Other graphs, such as pie charts, are also available.

The example could have been about the types of industries in a state, the kinds of automobiles produced at a plant, the kinds of services provided by a firm, or the kinds of goods sold in a store. The method of determining the frequencies would be the same in all such cases.

Relative Frequency for Qualitative Data

The magnitude of the frequency changes for different populations and samples. For better comparison, the relative frequency is used. The **relative frequency** shows the percentage of each class to the total population or sample. It is obtained by dividing the frequency for each class by the total in the population or the sample (see Table 1.4).

The sum of the relative frequency is always 1.0. Here, however, the sum is not exactly 1 due to roundoff error.

Graphical Methods for Qualitative Variables

The two most commonly used graphical methods for qualitative variables are bar graphs and pie charts. Many other graph types have been introduced with the advent of spreadsheet and more are available in specialty software.

Table 1.4. Business Types, Frequencies, and Relative Frequencies of Locations

Location	Frequency	Relative frequency
Gas Stations	3	0.1
Mechanic Shop	9	0.3
Drug Store	5	0.166
Hardware Store	7	0.233
Sporting Goods	4	0.133
School	1	0.033
Tire Shop	1	0.033
Total	30	0.9998

Bar Graph

A **bar graph** is a graphical representation of the frequency distribution, or relative frequency distribution, when dealing with qualitative data. The names of the qualitative variables are placed on the x-axis and the frequency is depicted on the y-axis. A **histogram** and a bar graph are identical except for the fact that the bar graph is used for qualitative variables, while the histogram is used for quantitative variables.

Example 1.2

The following table represents the frequency of the business type among 30 locations of soda dispensers. Provide a bar graph of the business types where soda dispensers are located.

Business type	Frequency
Gas Stations	3
Mechanic Shops	9
Drug Stores	5
Hardware Stores	7
Sporting Goods	4
School	1
Tire Shop	1
Total	30

Solution

All examples involving graphs are solved using Microsoft Office Excel. For the graphs, the appropriate Excel commands are given in each section. All the other Excel commands are included in the Appendix.

Bar graph in Excel is rotated 90° to the right. The sequence of commands to plot a bar graph in Excel is provided for your reference.

Open a new spreadsheet in Excel. In cell A1, type "Business Type" and then going downward list the business types as shown in the table above. In cell B1, type "Frequency" and then going downward list the

(Continued)

(*Continued*)

frequency in cells A1 through B8. Go to "Insert," which is the second tab at the top left on the spreadsheet. Click on "Column" (which looks like a bar graph) and then click on the first chart (top left). Excel will populate a chart similar to the one below.

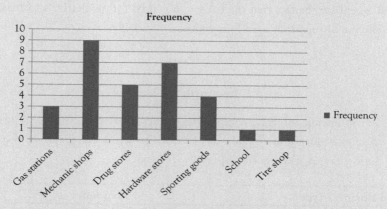

Figure 1.1. Bar graph of business types, frequencies, and relative frequencies of locations.

The above graph can represent the relative frequencies, too. Only the unit of measurement on the *y*-axis will differ. In Excel this graph is called a "column" graph.

Creating a bar graph of the relative frequencies would not provide additional meaningful results. The graph will be identical to the above graph, except the scales on the vertical axis would be the relative frequencies (percentages) and not the actual frequencies. However, the relative frequencies are already known so further benefit is not gained. Often it is more meaningful to plot the relative frequencies instead of the actual frequencies because you can easily compare relative frequencies and they are similar to probabilities.

Pie Chart

A pie chart is a graphical presentation of frequency distribution and relative frequency. In this regard, the pie chart is similar to the bar graph because one cannot differentiate between the graphs of actual and relative frequencies, except for the scale. In some cases when a quantitative variable has only few outcomes you can use the pie chart to provide visual effects.

A circle is divided into wedges representing each of the categories in the table. If frequencies are charted, their magnitude is placed under their name. When the pie chart is based on the relative frequencies instead of the frequencies, the scale will be different but not the size of the slices on the pie.

Example 1.3

Provide a pie graph for the business types of locations in Table 1.3.

Solution

Open a new spreadsheet in Excel. In cell A1, type "Business Type," list the business types as shown in the Table 1.3. In cell B1, type "Frequency" followed by the frequency for each business type as shown in the Table 1.3. Capture data in cells A1 through B8. Go to "Insert," which is the second tab at the top left hand corner of the spreadsheet. Click on "Pie." Several options become available. You can select whichever Pie shape you wish. Excel will populate a chart similar to the one below.

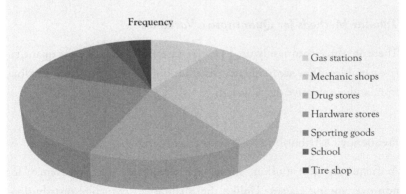

Figure 1.2. Pie charts of business types for soda dispensers—(Continued).

(*Continued*)

(*Continued*)

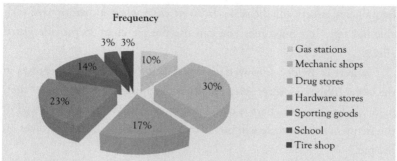

Figure 1.2. *Pie charts of business types for soda dispensers.*

Notice that due to space limitation the legend is placed on the side. Furthermore, the labels represent "Business Type" and have nothing to do with the pie colors the computer provides.

Descriptive Statistics for Quantitative Variables

As depicted in Table 1.1, there are more methods available to describe quantitative data. Some are very similar to the methods used in quantitative methods, but their interpretations are usually broader.

Tabular Methods for Quantitative Variables

There are three commonly used tabular descriptive statistics for quantitative variables. They are frequency distribution, relative frequency distribution, and cumulative distribution.

Frequency Distribution for Quantitative Variables

A frequency distribution shows the frequency of occurrence for non-overlapping classes. Unlike the qualitative frequency distribution, there are no set and predefined classes or groups. The researcher will determine the size of each class and the number of classes. Such data are called **grouped data**.

Example 1.4

An anthropologist is studying a small community of gold miners in a remote area. The community consists of nine families. The family income is reported below in thousands of dollars.

$$66, 58, 71, 73, 64, 70, 66, 55, 75$$

Solution

The researcher would like to summarize these data using descriptive statistics. We deliberately chose a small set to demonstrate the point better without boring calculations. In real life, data will be much larger, and it would make more sense to condense the data using some technique, say descriptive statistics. As only one value is repeated, it does not make sense to build a frequency distribution; no real summary will emerge. If we divide the data into classes, however, we can build the frequency distribution. The range of data is from 55 to 75. If the researcher wishes to have 5 classes, the size of each class would be:

$$\text{Class Width} = \frac{\text{Maximum} - \text{Minimum}}{\text{Number of Classes}} = \frac{75 - 55}{5} = 4$$

Table 1.5. Classes and Their Frequencies

Classes	Frequency
55–59	2
60–64	1
65–69	2
70–74	3
≥ 75	1

The number of classes is arbitrary and any reasonable number of classes and class widths will work. Avoid extremities and unbalanced classes. To avoid decimal places in classes, we added an extra class for values greater than or equal to 75. Other solutions would be as valid. The quantitative data can include decimal numbers; however, in this case, extra caution is needed to avoid overlapping in the classes.

The histogram command in Excel provides the frequency as well as the cumulative frequency. If the option "Chart Percentage" is selected from the histogram dialog box, the histogram and the **Ogive** will be graphed too.

A list of nine values has been reduced to a two-column table with six rows as shown in Table 1.5. Again here, the size of population is deliberately small to allow students to see the details easily and to be able to duplicate the results. The procedure would be the same for the family incomes of the United States with a population around 300,000,000 people. This signifies the power of statistics to condense information in as few parameters as possible. The result can be graphed for more visual presentation. One such graph is called a dot plot. Other graphs such as a histogram are also available.

Relative Frequency Distribution for Quantitative Variables

The relative frequency for quantitative variables is computed in the same way as those of qualitative variables. The frequency for each class is divided by the total number of members in the population or sample to obtain the relative frequency.

Example 1.5

Table 1.6 provides the relative and cumulative frequencies for the family incomes indicated in the Example 1.4.

Table 1.6. Relative and Cumulative Frequencies of Family Incomes

Classes	Frequency	Relative frequency	Cumulative frequency
55–59	2	0.222222222	0.222222222
60–64	1	0.111111111	0.333333333
65–69	2	0.222222222	0.555555556
70–74	3	0.333333333	0.888888889
≥ 75	1	0.111111111	1

Cumulative Frequency Distribution for Quantitative Variables

In the case of quantitative variables, the classes or values of interest are sequential and have meaningful order, usually from smallest to the largest. This allows us to obtain **cumulative frequencies**. Cumulative frequencies consist of sums of frequencies up to the value or class of interest. The last value is always 1 since it represents 100% of observations (see Table 1.6).

Percentiles

A **percentile** is the demarcation value below which the stated percentage of the population or sample lie. For example, 17% of a population or a sample lies below the 17th percentile.

To obtain a percentile, sort the data and identify which value represents the stated percentile. The 17th percentile of a data containing 84 members is the 15th member of the sorted group ($0.17 \times 84 = 14.28$). As countable data cannot take a fractional value, the 15th member of the sorted data is the observation where 17% of the data are smaller than it.

To obtain the percentile, after sorting the data calculate an index i:

$$i = \frac{p}{100} n \qquad (1.1)$$

where p is the desired percentile and n is either the population or the sample size. When the result is an integer, add 1 to it to get the position of the percentile. If the result is a decimal value, use the next higher integer to get the position of the percentile.

Example 1.6

A retail store has collected sales data, in thousands of dollars for 18 weeks. Find the 18th and the 50th percentiles for weekly sales.

66, 58, 71, 73, 64, 70, 66, 55, 75, 65, 57, 71, 72, 63, 71, 65, 55, 71

(Continued)

(*Continued*)

Solution

Sort the combined data.

$$55, 55, 57, 58, 63, 64, 65, 65, 66, 66, 70, 71, 71, 71, 71, 72, 73, 75$$

The 18th percentile is obtained by:

$$i = \frac{80}{100} \times 18 = 14.4$$

Since the result is a **real number**, it has decimal value. Thus, use the next higher integer, which is 15 in this example. The number in the 15th position is the 18th percentile. That value is 71.

The 50th percentile is:

$$i = \frac{50}{100} \times 18 = 9$$

Since the index is an integer, use the next higher integer, namely the 10th observation, which is 66.

Quartiles

Quartiles divide the population into four equal portions, each equal to 25% of the population. Like the median and percentiles, the data must be sorted first. The first quartile, Q_1, is the data point such that 25% of the data are below it. The second quartile, Q_2, is the data point such that 50% of the data are below it. The third quartile, Q_3, is the data point such that 75% of the data are below it.

The first quartile is the same as the 25th percentile. The second quartile is the same as the 50th percentile, as well as the median. The third quartile is the same as the 75th percentile. The quartiles are calculated the same way as the 25th, 50th, and 75th percentiles using the following indices.

Use $i = \frac{25}{100} \times n$ for the first quartile.

Use $i = \dfrac{50}{100} \times n$ for the second quartile.

Use $i = \dfrac{75}{100} \times n$ for the third quartile.

If the result of the index is an integer, use the next higher integer to find the location of the quartile. If the result of the index is a real value, a value with a decimal number, the next higher integer will determine the position of the quartile.

Example 1.7

For the weekly sales data of the retail store in Example 1.5, find the first, second, and the third percentiles. The data are repeated for your convenience.

66, 58, 71, 73, 64, 70, 66, 55, 75, 65, 57, 71, 72, 63, 71, 65, 55, 71

Solution

The 3 quartiles are calculated using the following indexes.

$i = \dfrac{25}{100} \times 18 = 4.5$ the first quartile is in the 5th position.

$i = \dfrac{50}{100} \times 18 = 9$ the second quartile is in the 10th position.

$i = \dfrac{75}{100} \times 18 = 13.5$ the third quartile is in the 14th position.

Sort the combined data.

55, 55, 57, 58, 63, 64, 65, 65, 66, 66, 70, 71, 71, 71, 71, 72, 73, 75

Q_1 Q_2 Q_3

Definition 1.11

The first quartile is the 25th percentile, the second quartile is the 50th percentile, and the third quartile is the 75th percentile.

Hinges

The hinges also divide the data into four equal portions. The hinges, however, use the definition of the median. For example, sort the data (as indicated below) and then find the median. Find the median of the lower half and call it the first hinge. Find the median of the second half and call it the upper hinge.

Example 1.8

For the weekly sales data of the retail store in Example 1.5, find the first, second, and third percentiles.

Solution

Sort the combined data.

55, 55, 57, 58, **63**, 64, 65, 65, 66, 66, 70, 71, 71, **71**, 71, 72, 73, 75
              lower hinge   Median   upper hinge

Graphical Methods for Quantitative Variables

The numbers of available graphical methods for quantitative variables far exceed the number of graphical methods available for qualitative variables. Here, we will address histograms, Ogive, stem-and-leaf, dot-plot, scatter plot, and box plot. Box plot uses some of the concepts that are introduced in Chapter 2.

Histogram

A histogram is a graphical representation of the frequency distribution or relative frequency distribution when dealing with quantitative data. The boundaries of the classes are used for the demarcation of the vertical bars. A histogram and a bar graph are identical except for the quantitative values used in the histogram on the x-axis.

Example 1.9

The following data represents the income of gold miners in a small community. The corresponding histogram follows (see Figure 1.3).

Classes	Frequency
55–59	2
60–64	1
65–69	2
70–74	3
≥75	1

Open a new spreadsheet in Excel. In cell A1, type "Bin" and enter the Bin Range from the list below. In cell B1, type "Frequency" followed by the frequencies. The data should be captured in cells A1 through B6. Go to "Insert," which is the second tab at the top left hand corner of the spreadsheet. Click on "Column" (which looks like a bar graph) and then click on the first chart (top left). Excel will populate a chart similar to the one below.

The output from Excel is presented below. The frequency is shown too.

55	Bin Range
58	59
64	64
66	69
66	74
70	
71	
73	
75	

Bin	Frequency
59	2
64	1
69	2
74	3
More	1

Figure 1.3. Histogram and related setup in Excel—(Continued)

(*Continued*)

(*Continued*)

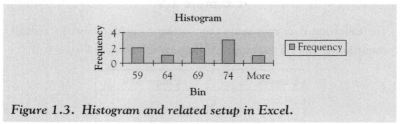

Figure 1.3. Histogram and related setup in Excel.

The above graph can represent the relative frequencies, too. Only the unit of measurement on the *y*-axis will differ.

The above graph was created in Excel. Ironically, in Excel this graph is called a "column" graph. Bar graph in Excel is the same thing except for the rotation of 90° to the right.

Ogive

The graph for the cumulative frequencies is called Ogive. In carpentry, there is a molding bit for shaping the edge of the wood called Roman Ogive. The graphs of the cumulative frequencies usually resemble the finished edge of the Roman Ogive molding.

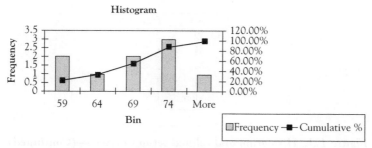

Figure 1.4. Ogive superimposed on histogram.

Example 1.10

For the below nine communities of gold miners, find the graph frequencies and cumulative frequencies.

$$66, 58, 71, 73, 64, 70, 66, 55, 75$$

Solution

The frequency, relative frequency, and cumulative frequency for these data are given in Table 1.7.

Table 1.7. Frequency, Relative Frequency, and Cumulative Frequency

Classes	Frequency	Relative frequency	Cumulative frequency
55–59	2	0.222	0.222
60–64	1	0.111	0.333
65–69	2	0.222	0.555
70–75	4	0.444	0.999

In Excel the Ogive is obtained from the histogram dialog box by selecting the cumulative percentage option.

The Ogive gives the cumulative area under the relative frequency histogram. The derivative of the function that represents the Ogive will give the relative frequency histogram function (see Figure 1.4).

Stem-and-Leaf

Stem-and-leaf is another descriptive way of summarizing information and, hence, qualifies as descriptive statistics. Tukey[3] introduced the concepts of the stem-and-leaf. Some authors, such as Anderson *et al.*,[4] place stem-and-leaf under the exploratory data.

In the stem-and-leaf, usually the last digit of a value is recorded as the leaf and the preceding digits on a number as the stem.

A vertical line for easy visualization separates the leaves and stems. To create a stem-and-leaf display, place the first digit(s) of each data to the left of a vertical line. Place the last digit of each data to the right of the line.

Example 1.11

Provide a stem-and-leaf graph for the gold miners' data.

$$66, 58, 71, 73, 64, 70, 66, 55, 75$$

Solution

The frequency, relative frequency, and cumulative frequency for this data are given in Table 1.7.

```
6 | 6  4  6
5 | 8  5
7 | 0  1  3  5
```

Figure 1.5(a). Stem-and-leaf graph.

Note that the result resembles a rotated histogram. If the data for each leaf is also sorted, a better summary is obtained, as in Figure 1.5(b).

```
6 | 4  4  6
5 | 5  8
7 | 0  1  3  5
```

Figure 1.5(b). Sorted stem-and-leaf graph.

If the numbers are too large, the first two or more digits could be placed on the left side. The idea is to select the digits in a manner that makes the summary useful.

Dot Plot

The dot plot is useful when only one set of data is under consideration. The actual data are placed on the x-axis. For each occurrence of the value a dot is placed above it. All the dots are at the same height, which has no significant meaning other than reflecting the occurrence of the observation. In the case of multiple occurrences additional dots are placed above the previous ones. The dots are placed at equal distances for visual as well as representation purpose.

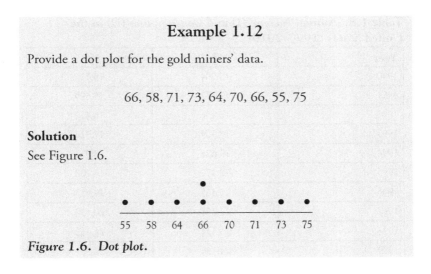

Example 1.12

Provide a dot plot for the gold miners' data.

$$66, 58, 71, 73, 64, 70, 66, 55, 75$$

Solution
See Figure 1.6.

Figure 1.6. Dot plot.

A dot plot resembles an exaggerated histogram.

Scatter Plot

An observant reader would notice that all the previous examples have been based on only one variable with numerous classifications and categories. In economics and many other branches of science, it is also beneficial to present graphics of two or more variables. Below, we will use a scatter plot to show the relationship between two variables (see Figure 1.7). More variables can be combined into one graph. Usually, numerous variables are placed on the x-axis and only one variable is placed on the y-axis to show the relationship between the variable in the former group and the variable on the y-axis. In such cases, the variables on the x-axis are usually the ones that affect the variable on the y-axis. Sometimes they are called **factors** and **response** variables, respectively.

Example 1.13

Graph a scatter plot of annual income and consumption data for the United States for the years 1990 through 2010 which is depicted in Table 1.8.

Table 1.8. Annual Income (I) and Consumption (C) in the United States (1990–2010)

Year	I	C
1990	17,004	15,331
1991	17,532	15,699
1992	18,436	16,491
1993	18,909	17,226
1994	19,678	18,033
1995	20,470	18,708
1996	21,355	19,553
1997	22,255	20,408
1998	23,534	21,432
1999	24,356	22,707
2000	25,944	24,185
2001	26,805	25,054
2002	27,799	25,819
2003	28,805	26,833
2004	30,287	28,179
2005	31,318	29,719
2006	33,157	31,102
2007	34,512	32,356
2008	36,166	32,922
2009	35,088	32,087
2010	36,051	33,039

Sources: Bureau of Economic Analysis: National Income and Product Account Tables (Table 2.3.5-Personal Consumption Expenditures by Major Type of Product). GDP and Personal Income (SA1-3 Personal Income Summary).

(*Continued*)

Solution

To obtain a scatter plot, type the information from Table 1.8 in an Excel spreadsheet. In cell A1 type "I" for Income followed by the income data from the second column in Table 1.8. In cell B1, type "C" for Consumption followed by consumption data from the third column in Table 1.8. Highlight cells A1 through B22. Go to "Insert," which is the second tab on the top left hand corner of the spreadsheet. Click on "Scatter," which will reveal several options. Select the option at the top left. Excel will populate a chart similar to the one shown in Figure 1.7.

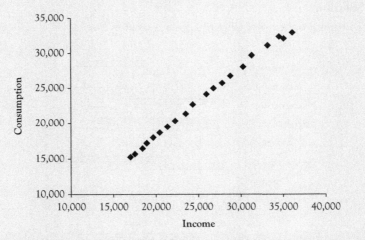

Figure 1.7. Scatter plot of income and consumption for the United States, 1990–2010.

These graphs present, by no means, the extent of possible ways to present data for either qualitative or quantitative variables. Many other imaginative ways can be used, some of which are available in popular software such as Microsoft Excel or dedicated software such as Stata.

Box Plot

A box plot is a visual representation of several basic descriptive statistics in a concise manner. The descriptive statistics that are used in a box plot are explained in Chapter 2. The graph consists of one box per variable. The borders of the box represent the 25th percentile (**lower hinge**) and

the 75th percentile (**upper hinge**), with a line in the box representing
the 50th percentile or the median. Lines, called whiskers, extend from the
edges of the box to the *adjacent* values, capped by an **adjacent line**.[5] The
values further away from the box extending past the adjacent lines in
either direction are called **outside values**.

Example 1.14

Use the data from Table 1.2 to obtain the box plot of income by the
type of business and by gender.

Solution
The graph of box plot (Figure 1.8) is created in Stata.

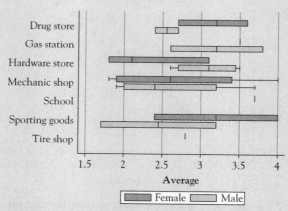

Figure 1.8. Box plot of income by location and by gender.

CHAPTER 2

Numerical Descriptive Statistics for Quantitative Variables

Introduction

One of the purposes of descriptive statistics is to summarize the information in the data for a variable into as few **parameters** as possible. **Measures of central tendency** provide concise meaningful summaries of the population. Measures of central tendency are addressed in the below section. However, measures of central tendency are often not enough to provide the full picture. The addition of **measures of dispersion** provides a more complete picture. Measures of dispersion are covered in next, followed by **measures of association.**

Measures of Central Tendency

Mean

The arithmetic mean, or simply the mean, is the most commonly used descriptive measure. Other names for the mean are average, mathematical expectation, and the expected value. This section deals with raw or ungrouped data.

Arithmetic Mean

The mean takes the concept of condensing information to the extreme. The mean, a single value, is the **representative** or **typical value** that represents a population. The mean is also known as the **average**, and more formally as the **expected value**. The mean is the sum of all the elements in the population divided by the number of the elements.

$$\mu = \frac{\sum_{i=1}^{N} X_i}{N} \qquad (2.1)$$

where μ, pronounced mu, is the symbol used to represent the mean; Σ, pronounced sigma, represents the sum of some random variables. When there is no ambiguity, we can simply write:

$$\mu = \frac{\Sigma(X)}{N} \qquad (2.2)$$

The mean is a parameter and provides information about the central tendency of the population. The mean is the representative, or expected value, of the population. For example, when we say that the average income of a country is \$45,000, we are stating that if a person is selected at random his income is expected to be around \$45,000. The mean is the expected value or the typical representative of a population when there is no other information.

The mean, though being the most widely used and most important parameter of the population, has its limits. It is susceptible to extreme values. Since all values of the population are used in calculation of the mean, a single very large or very small value can have a major impact on it. This is not quite as important in the case of the population as it is with samples.

Sample Mean

The sample mean is the sum of the sample values divided by the sample size.

$$\hat{\mu} = \bar{X} = \frac{\Sigma(X)}{n} \qquad (2.3)$$

Note that we used both, $\hat{\mu}$, pronounced mu-hat, and $\bar{X}$, pronounced x-bar to represent the sample mean. Both are widely accepted. However, $\hat{\mu}$ has several advantages over $\bar{X}$. The first advantage is that it reduces the number of symbols that one has to learn in half. The population parameter is μ and its estimate $\hat{\mu}$. The second advantage is that it takes the guesswork out of which statistics you are dealing with, as long as you remember the population parameter. The third advantage is that it provides a reasonably simple rule to follow. Population parameters are represented by Greek letters, and sample statistics are represented by Greek letters with a hat on them.

Definition 2.1

Statistics is a numeric fact or summary obtained from a sample. It is always known, because it is calculated by the researcher and it is a variable. Statistics is also used to make inferences about the corresponding population parameter.

The sample mean is a statistic. It is used to estimate the population parameter μ.

Example 2.1

An anthropologist is studying a small community of gold miners in a remote area. The community consists of nine families. The family income is reported below in thousands of dollars. Find the sample mean. This data is hypothetical, but plausible. We use this data to show computational detail.

$$66, 58, 71, 73, 64, 70, 66, 55, 75$$

Solution
A careful reader would remember that the same data and scenario was introduced in Example 1.4 but with a major difference. The data there was presented as population data. The idea of a small community with nine families is acceptable but a sample of nine is more plausible. We are using the same data for ease of computation and we limit the data size to avoid tedious computations. Nevertheless, we use actual data with more observations in different parts of the texts as well.

(Continued)

(Continued)

The sample mean is:

$$\hat{\mu} = \bar{X} = \frac{66+58+71+73+64+70+66+55+75}{9} = \frac{598}{9} = 66.444$$

The expected income (in thousands of dollars) of any family from this population is 66.444. This statistic is an estimate of the population parameter μ.

We did not provide an example for the population mean because most populations are large and it would take a lot of space to display such a vast amount of data. In addition, we were concerned that you would not see the forest for the trees. The procedure is nevertheless the same. We can assume that the above data is actually the population and obtain the mean, which would be the same number. However, there is a major difference between the sample mean and population mean, as between any **statistics** and **parameter**. The former is a variable while the latter is a constant. In actual research we seldom, if ever, know population parameters, which necessitate collecting samples and obtaining sample statistics to make inference about the **unknown** population **parameters**. It is possible to have a small population, for example, the population can consist of the two children in a household but usually they are of little use in economic studies.

If one of few extreme members of the population appears in a sample, especially a small sample, the impact will be detrimental. Remember the sample mean, a statistics, is used to estimate the population mean, a parameter. If the sample mean is erroneous, the estimated population mean will be misleading. Irrespective of what values appear in the sample, the sample mean does provide an unbiased estimate of the population mean.

Example 2.2

The stock prices for Wal-Mart and Microsoft for the period from March 12 to March 30, 2012 and April 2 to April 21, 2012 are provided in Table 2.1. We will use these data in many of the examples in this book.

(Continued)

Table 2.1. Closing Prices of Wal-Mart (WMT) and Microsoft (MSFT) for the period from March 12 to March 30 and from April 2 to April 21, 2012

Date	WMT	MSFT	Date	WMT	MSFT
12 Mar.	$60.68	$32.04	2 Apr.	$61.36	$32.29
13 Mar.	$61.00	$32.67	3 Apr.	$60.65	$31.94
14 Mar.	$61.08	$32.77	4 Apr.	$60.26	$31.21
15 Mar.	$61.23	$32.85	5 Apr.	$60.67	$31.52
16 Mar.	$60.84	$32.60	9 Apr.	$60.13	$31.10
19 Mar.	$60.74	$32.20	10 Apr.	$59.93	$30.47
20 Mar.	$60.60	$31.99	11 Apr.	$59.80	$30.35
21 Mar.	$60.56	$31.91	12 Apr.	$60.14	$30.98
22 Mar.	$60.65	$32.00	13 Apr.	$59.77	$30.81
23 Mar.	$60.75	$32.01	16 Apr.	$60.58	$31.08
26 Mar.	$61.20	$32.59	17 Apr.	$61.87	$31.44
27 Mar.	$61.09	$32.52	18 Apr.	$62.06	$31.14
28 Mar.	$61.19	$32.19	19 Apr.	$61.75	$31.01
29 Mar.	$60.82	$32.12	20 Apr.	$62.45	$32.42
30 Mar.	$61.20	$32.26	21 Apr.	$59.54	$32.12

Find the (sample) average price for Wal-Mart for the period from April 2 to April 21, 2012.

Solution

$$\hat{\mu} = \bar{X} = \frac{\Sigma(X)}{n} = \frac{910.96}{15} = \$60.73$$

Example 2.3

Suppose the researcher in Example 2.1 collected another sample: The income of these new families is reported below. The researcher wants to calculate the sample mean of their income as well.

$$65, 57, 71, 72, 63, 71, 65, 55, 71$$

Solution

$$\hat{\mu} = \bar{X} = \frac{590}{9} = 65.555\bar{5}$$

The sample mean changed since it is a statistic, which is a variable. This sample mean provides an estimate of the population mean μ. Usually, the parameter remains unknown and statistics provide estimates of it. The mean of combined population can be obtained from the separate component population means. If the researcher considers the 18 observations (of Examples 2.1 and 2.3) as one sample, the sample mean would be:

$$\hat{\mu} = \bar{X} = \frac{1188}{18} = 66$$

The same result can be obtained from previous information:

$$\hat{\mu}_1 = \bar{X}_1 = 66.4444 \quad \text{and} \quad \hat{\mu}_2 = \bar{X}_2 = 65.5555.$$

The mean of the combined samples is:

$$\hat{\mu} = \bar{X} = \frac{66.4444 + 65.555}{2} = 66$$

In this case, the sample sizes are equal, so simple arithmetic average works fine. In the case of different sample sizes, the **weighted average** is the appropriate tool.

Later, we will cover two other measures of central tendency called **median** and **mode**. The knowledge of the **median** or the **mode** of two samples or two populations do not render to such calculation. The median or the mode of combined populations or samples cannot be obtained from the component populations or samples.

Trimmed Mean

Trimmed mean is a modification of the mean. The sample data is sorted and a given percentage, say 5%, of the top and the bottom of the data are discarded, and the regular mean is calculated for the remaining data. This trimmed mean will be less susceptible to the extreme values.

Geometric Mean

The geometric mean is calculated using the following formula.

$$\text{GM} = \sqrt[N]{X_1 X_2 \dots X_N} \tag{2.4}$$

In logarithmic form

$$\text{Log(GM)} = \frac{1}{N}\sum_{i=1}^{N}\log(X_i) = \frac{\log(X_1)+\log(X_2)+\cdots+\log(X_N)}{N} \quad (2.5)$$

The advantage of the logarithmic formula is that it avoids taking the root of the results. This was more important before the advent of powerful calculators. The logarithmic formula is a linear sum of its elements. After taking the logarithm of the values the mean is calculated as the arithmetic mean.

The geometric mean is useful when the values change in geometric progression instead of arithmetic progression, as is the case with growth rates.

Example 2.4

Assume that a new company grew at 28% the first year, 15% the second year, and 13% the third year. What is the rate of the growth of company?

1st year	1.00	beginning of the operation
2nd year	1.28	28% increase over the beginning
3rd year	1.472	15% increase over the 2nd year
4th year	1.66336	13% increase over the 3rd year

The arithmetic mean is not able to explain the geometric growth. The geometric mean will give the average.

$$GM = \sqrt[3]{1.28\times1.472\times1.66336} = \sqrt[3]{3.134036378} = 1.463416715$$

The company grew at the average rate of 1.4634 or 46.34% per year.
Raise both sides to the 3rd power.

$$3.134036378 = (1.463416715)^3 = (1+0.463476715)^3$$

This is the formula for compound interest. To generalize, let P_0 be the initial investment, P_n the amount after n years, and r the interest rate or the rate of growth.

(*Continued*)

(Continued)

$$P_n = P_0(1 + r)^n \tag{2.6}$$

In the example the ending value is known to be $P_n = 3.134036378$, the beginning value is $P_0 = 1.0$, and $n = 3$. The (average) rate of growth is

$$3.134036378 = 1.0\,(1 + r)^3$$

$$(1 + r) = \sqrt[3]{3.134036378} = 1.463416715$$

$$r = 1.463416715 - 1 = 0.463416715$$

Therefore, the (average) rate of growth is 46.34%, as was derived from the geometric mean.

The geometric mean is also the proper mean when dealing with **ratio** of items.

Example 2.5

The ratio of the average income to the price of an average car is 4 in year 1 and 5 in year 2. What is the average ratio of income to the price of a car?

Solution

Using the arithmetic mean of income to car price provides an incorrect answer:

$$(4 + 5)/2 = 4.5$$

The arithmetic mean of car price to income

$$= \frac{\left(\dfrac{1}{4} + \dfrac{1}{5}\right)}{2} = \frac{(0.25 + 0.2)}{2} = 0.225$$

The reciprocal of 0.225 is $(1/0.225) = 4.444$ not 4.5. Therefore, the arithmetic mean is not a suitable measure when dealing with ratios.

(Continued)

The average of the ratio of income to car price should not differ from the average of the ratio of the car price to income.

The geometric mean for the two ratios is:

Geometric mean of income to car price = $\sqrt{4 \times 5} = \sqrt{20}$
Geometric mean of car price to income = $\sqrt{0.25 \times 0.2} = \sqrt{0.05}$

The reciprocal of $\sqrt{0.05}$ is $\left(1 / \sqrt{0.05}\right) + \sqrt{20}$. Since the geometric mean of the income to the price of car is the same as the reciprocal of the geometric mean of the price of car to income, the geometric mean is the proper average measure.

Harmonic Mean

The harmonic mean is calculated using the following formula.

$$HM = \frac{N}{\sum\limits_{i=1}^{N} \frac{1}{X_i}} = \frac{N}{\frac{1}{X_1} + \frac{1}{X_2} + \cdots + \frac{1}{X_N}} \tag{2.7}$$

The harmonic mean is, in fact, the reciprocal of the arithmetic mean of the reciprocal of the values.

Example 2.6

A salesman travels to another city to meet a client. To make sure that he does not miss the appointment, he drives at 90 miles per hour. After a successful meeting he returns more leisurely at 45 miles per hour. What was his average speed?

Solution
The speed was not $(90 + 45)/2 = 67.5$ mile per hour. For simplicity, assume he traveled a distance of 90 miles (any other value will work as well).

(*Continued*)

(*Continued*)

$$\text{Time while going} = \frac{90}{90} = 1$$

$$\text{Time while returning} = \frac{90}{45} = 2$$

$$\text{Total travel time} = 1 + 2 = 3$$

$$\text{Average speed} = \frac{Distance}{Time} = \frac{90 + 90}{1 + 2} = 60 = 60 \text{ miles per hour}$$

The harmonic mean will give the correct answer where the arithmetic mean failed.

$$\text{HM} = \frac{2}{\dfrac{1}{90} + \dfrac{1}{45}} = \frac{2}{\dfrac{1+2}{90}} = \frac{2 \times 90}{3} = 60 \text{ miles per hour}$$

Rule 2.1

When n = 2 the geometric mean is equal to the square root of the arithmetic mean times the harmonic mean.

$$GM = \sqrt{(AM)(HM)} \tag{2.8}$$

Mean for Data with Frequencies

The expanded presentation below will be revealing.

$$\mu = \frac{X_1 + X_2 + \cdots + X_N}{N} = \frac{X_1}{N} + \frac{X_2}{N} + \cdots + \frac{X_N}{N}$$
$$= \frac{1}{N} X_1 + \frac{1}{N} X_2 + \cdots + \frac{1}{N} X_N \tag{2.9}$$

The mean is the sum of $1/N$ times of each observation. In other words, each observation gets a weight equal to $1/N$ of the total. Sometimes, each value should receive a different weight, say, $f_1, f_2, \ldots, f_N$ for each of $X_1, X_2, \ldots, X_N$. In that case the result is in terms of frequencies of each value.

$$\mu = f_1 X_1 + f_2 X_2 + \cdots + f_N X_N = \Sigma f X \tag{2.10}$$

Note that $\Sigma f = 1$ and, hence, was not written. In general, the formula for the frequencies would be:

$$\mu = \frac{f_1 X_1 + f_2 X_2 + \cdots + f_N X_N}{f_1 + f_2 + \cdots + f_N} \quad (2.11)$$

Weighted Mean

The weighted mean is similar to the mean using the frequencies, except that the sum of weights need not add up to one.

$$\mu = \frac{w_1 X_1 + w_2 X_2 + \cdots + w_N X_N}{w_1 + w_2 + \cdots + w_N} \quad (2.12)$$

Example 2.7

Refer to Example 2.1 and Example 2.3 regarding the incomes of gold miners from two samples.

$$66, 58, 71, 73, 64, 70, 66, 55, 75$$
$$65, 57, 71, 72, 63, 71, 65, 55, 71$$

List the data according to incomes and their frequencies in a table. Use the number of cases, which is the same as frequencies in this example, as weight and calculate the weighted average.

Solution
This example is exactly the same as Example 2.8, except in the way the number of times an income is named. Here, they are considered as weights for each observation while in Example 2.8 they are considered frequencies.

Recall that the sample mean for the 18 men is

$$\hat{\mu} = \frac{1188}{18} = 66$$

The mean obtained by using the frequency distribution shown in the following table should be the same.

(Continued)

(*Continued*)

Observation	Weights
55	2
57	1
58	1
63	1
64	1
65	2
66	2
70	1
71	4
72	1
73	1
75	1
Total	18

Adding up the observations and dividing by 12 will give an incorrect answer, except for coincidence. To obtain the correct mean, each observation must be multiplied by the number of times it occurs.

Note that the sum for the population is over the population size N, while the sum for the sample is for the sample size n.

$$\hat{\mu} = \frac{55 \times 2 + 57 \times 1 + 58 \times 1 + 63 \times 1 + 64 \times 1 + 65 \times 2 + 66 \times 2 + 70 \times 1 + 71 \times 4 + 72 \times 1 + 73 \times 1 + 75 \times 1}{18}$$

$$\hat{\mu} = \frac{1188}{18} = 66$$

Relation Between Arithmetic, Geometric, and Harmonic Mean

$$HM \leq GM \leq \mu \tag{2.13}$$

The equality sign holds only if all sample values are identical.

Mean of Grouped Data

Statistics is the science of summarizing information. This goal is attained at several stages. The frequency distribution is a tabular summary of data. The mean is another summary statistics that is much more powerful in representing the data. Often, the data are only available after being summarized as frequency distribution. In those cases, it is desirable to be able to find the mean and other valuable parameters.

Mean of Data Summarized as Frequencies

The formula for the population mean is:

$$\mu = \frac{\sum_{i=1}^{N} f_i X_i}{\sum_{i=1}^{N} f_i} \qquad (2.14)$$

The formula for the sample mean is:

$$\hat{\mu} = \frac{\sum_{i=1}^{n} f_i X_i}{\sum_{i=1}^{n} f_i} \qquad (2.15)$$

Example 2.8

Refer to Example 2.1 and Example 2.3 regarding the incomes of gold miners from two samples.

$$66, 58, 71, 73, 64, 70, 66, 55, 75$$
$$65, 57, 71, 72, 63, 71, 65, 55, 71$$

List the data according to incomes and their frequencies in a table. Calculate the mean using the values and their frequencies.

Solution

Using the table from Example 2.7 and multiplying the observations with the frequencies, we have

$$\hat{\mu} = \frac{55\times2+57\times1+58\times1+63\times1+64\times1+65\times2+66\times2+70\times1+71\times4+72\times1+73\times1+75\times1}{18}$$

$$\hat{\mu} = \frac{1188}{18} = 66$$

Therefore, summarizing the data into a frequency distribution does not affect the mean. It does not affect the **variance** either. The mean of the grouped data, however, will most likely be different than the actual mean. This is due partly to the fact that the class sizes are arbitrary, and mostly due to the formula.

Mean for Grouped Data

The formula for the mean of the population grouped data is:

$$\mu = \frac{\Sigma fM}{\Sigma f} \qquad (2.16)$$

The formula for the mean of the sample grouped data is:

$$\hat{\mu} = \frac{\Sigma fM}{\Sigma f}, \qquad (2.17)$$

where M is the mid-point of each class. Once again the only difference between the population and sample formulas is in the number of elements and where they originate. This is the same as the weighted mean where the weights are the frequencies. Each value is given a weight equal to its number of occurrences or frequency.

Example 2.9

Group the data from Example 2.1 into four groups, each representing a 5-year interval. Calculate the mean using the grouped data.

Solution

Classes	Frequency	M
55–59	4	57
60–64	2	62
65–69	4	67
70–75	8	72.5

(Continued)

$$\hat{\mu} = \frac{4 \times 57 + 2 \times 62 + 4 \times 67 + 8 \times 72.5}{18}$$

$$= \frac{228 + 124 + 268 + 580}{18} = 66.6667$$

The result has changed slightly. Other groupings will result in different calculated means.

Quartiles

Quartiles divide data into quarters. The first quartile is such a number that 24% of data are below it. Similarly, 50% of data are below the second quartile and 75% are below the third quartile. To obtain quartiles, sort the data and find 1 quarter, 2 quarters, and 3 quarters demarcations. See Examples 2.10 and 2.13 for numerical solutions.

Median

The median is such a value greater than 50% of the population. To obtain the median, sort the data—the one in the middle is the median. If there are two numbers at the middle, their average is the median. Some texts use M to designate the median. The median is the same as the 50th **per-centile,** as well as the **second quartile**.

Example 2.10

Refer to Example 2.1 and Example 2.3 regarding the incomes of the gold miners in two communities. Calculate the median for each community separately. Find the median for combined data.

66, 58, 71, 73, 64, 70, 66, 55, 75
65, 57, 71, 72, 63, 71, 65, 55, 71

(Continued)

(Continued)

Solution

To obtain the median of each group, sort the values first. The medians for the following two data sets are in bold letters.

55, 58, 64, 66, **66**, 70, 71, 73, 75
55, 57, 63, 65, **65**, 71, 71, 71, 72

The median of combined population cannot be obtained from the separate component population medians.

55, 55, 57, 58, 63, 64, 65, 65, 66, 66, 70, 71, 71, 71, 71, 72, 73, 75

The median is $(66 + 66)/2 = 66$.

Mode

The mode is another measure of central tendency. The mode is the most frequently occurring value of the population. A population, or a sample, may have more than one mode or no mode at all. If all members of the population occur as frequently, either no mode is present or every element is a mode. If there are two modes, the distribution is called bimodal. When the incomes of men and women are measured, there will be two modes, one for men and another for women.

Example 2.11

For data in Example 2.1 and Example 2.3, obtain the mode for the incomes of the two communities. Find the mode for the combined data as well.

Solution

66, 58, 71, 73, 64, 70, 66, 55, 75
65, 57, 71, 72, 63, 71, 65, 55, 71

The mode for the first community is 66, and for the second community is 71. From the frequency distribution table provided in Example 2.7 the mode for the combined data is 71.

The mode of combined population cannot be obtained from the separate component population modes. When the data is grouped, the mode is the midpoint of the interval with the greatest frequency. In a bar graph or a histogram, the tallest bar represents the modal value. In this case the range 70–75 years is the mode.

Empirical Relation Between Mean, Median, and Mode

$$\text{Mean} - \text{Mode} = 3 \, (\text{Mean} - \text{Median}) \qquad (2.18)$$

Measures of Dispersion

Range

The range is a measure of dispersion. It reflects how far the data are scattered. It is calculated by subtracting the minimum value from the maximum value.

$$R = \text{Maximum} - \text{Minimum} \qquad (2.19)$$

Example 2.12

For the data in Example 2.1 and Example 2.3, obtain the range for the combined data.

$$66, 58, 71, 73, 64, 70, 66, 55, 75$$
$$65, 57, 71, 72, 63, 71, 65, 55, 71$$

Solution
$$R = 75 - 55 = 20$$

Interquartile Range

The interquartile range is a measure of dispersion that measures the distance between the first and the third quartiles.

$$IQR = Q_3 - Q_1 \qquad (2.20)$$

Example 2.13

For the data in Example 2.1 and Example 2.3, obtain the interquartile range for the combined data.

$$66, 58, 71, 73, 64, 70, 66, 55, 75$$
$$65, 57, 71, 72, 63, 71, 65, 55, 71$$

Solution

Combine and sort the data.

55, 55, 57, 58, **63**, 64, 65, 65, 66, **66**, 70, 71, 71, **71**, 71, 72, 73, 75
$\qquad\qquad Q_1 \qquad\qquad\qquad\qquad Q_2 \qquad\qquad\qquad Q_3$

IQR = 71 − 63 = 12

The IQR can be used to find the "middle class" of a population or a sample. It gives the lower and upper limits of the middle 50%.

Variance

The variance is a measure of dispersion. It is one of the more important parameters of a population. The concept of variance is used in many aspects of statistics.

The variance is the average error, squared. The need for the variance arises from the need to determine and calculate the error, which is an important statistical measure. The population mean is the best representative of the population. It represents the typical value or the expected value of any member of the population. Seldom, however, every member of the population has the identical value. If they did there would not be any point in studying and analyzing them. Each member of the population will be off from the expected value by some magnitude. The deviation may be positive or negative. Understanding and analyzing the individual errors would be difficult. Instead, the average error is used. As with other subjects in statistics, the goal is to reduce the phenomena to as few parameters as possible.

This section deals with the raw or ungrouped data. The total error and, hence, the average error is always equal to zero. As a mathematical property $\Sigma(X - \mu) = 0$. To overcome this problem the deviations are squared to obtain:

$$\Sigma(X - \mu)^2$$

This value cannot be zero unless every observation is identical. Since larger populations will have larger sum of squared deviation, their average is calculated to enable comparison of different sized populations.

Population Variance

The variance is the sum of the squares of the deviations of values from their mean, divided by population size. Therefore, the variance is the mean of the squared deviations, which in the case of a sample it is called the mean squared error (MSE) and, hence, is an average measure. The variance is the entire variation in a population. It does not change.

$$\sigma^2 = \frac{\Sigma(X - \mu)^2}{N} \tag{2.21}$$

The variance is also called "sigma squared" to reflect the fact that it is a squared measure. The variance reflects (the square of) how much a data point can deviate from the expected value, that is, the mean for the data. The numerator, the sum of squares of deviations, is usually called sum of squared total (SST).

Sample Variance

The sample variance is the sum of the squares of the deviations of values from the sample mean divided by the **degrees of freedom**. The concept of degrees of freedom is discussed in Chapter 3. The sample variance represents the entire variation in a given sample. Sample variance does not change for a given sample. As sample variance is a statistic, its value will change from one sample to the other.

$$\widehat{\sigma^2} = \frac{\Sigma(X - \widehat{\mu_X})^2}{n - 1} \tag{2.22}$$

Example 2.14

Refer to the gold miners income data of Example 2.1 and Example 2.3:

$$66, 58, 71, 73, 64, 70, 66, 55, 75$$
$$65, 57, 71, 72, 63, 71, 65, 55, 71$$

Calculate the sample variances of the incomes for each community.

Solution

The sample variance for the first community is calculated as follows:

Income	$(X - \hat{\mu})$	$(X - \hat{\mu})^2$
66	−0.44444	0.197531
58	−8.44444	71.30864
71	4.555556	20.75309
73	6.555556	42.97531
64	−2.44444	5.975309
70	3.555556	12.64198
66	−0.44444	0.197531
55	−11.4444	130.9753
75	8.555556	73.19753

$$\widehat{\sigma^2} = \frac{\Sigma(X - \widehat{\mu_X})^2}{n-1} = \frac{358.2222}{8} = 44.7778$$

Similarly, the sample variance for the second community is calculated and is equal to

$$\widehat{\sigma^2} = 40.277778$$

Verify that the variance of the combined samples is neither the sum of the variances of the samples, nor the average of their variances. You can also easily verify that the sum of $(X - \hat{\mu})$ equals zero, which will be useful in later discussions.

Standard Deviation

The variance, of the population or sample, is in the square of the unit of the measurement of the observation. To make them comparable to the actual observation their square roots is taken.

$$\sigma = \sqrt{\frac{\Sigma(X - \mu)^2}{N}} \tag{2.23}$$

The σ is called the **standard deviation**. Its counterpart is called **sample standard deviation** and is denoted by $\hat{\sigma}$, pronounced sigma hat.

$$\hat{\sigma} = \sqrt{\frac{\Sigma(X - \widehat{\mu_X})^2}{n - 1}} \tag{2.24}$$

The standard deviation represents the **average error** of a population or sample. The standard deviation is a measure of risk, too. It reflects how much a data point can deviate from the expected value, that is, the mean of the data, by chance. The standard deviation is the statistical "yardstick" that allows comparison of dissimilar entities. To measure the length of a room, place a yardstick at one end of the room; mark the floor at the end of the yardstick, move the yardstick to the mark, and mark the floor at the end of yardstick again, until the entire length of the room is measured. In other words, you divide the length of the room by the length of the yardstick, and the result will be a value in terms of the yard. The divisor provides the unit of measurement. Hence, the unit of measurement of standardized values is standard deviation.

The Standard Deviation of the Sample Mean

When the value under consideration is the **sample mean**, its distribution is explained by the **sampling distribution of the sample mean**, a topic which is covered in detail in Chapter 5. For the time being, we will simply provide the relationship without the background information:

$$\mathrm{Var}(\hat{\mu}) = \sigma_{\hat{\mu}}^2 = \frac{\sigma^2}{n} \tag{2.25}$$

If the population variance is not known, replace it with the sample variance:

$$\mathrm{Var}(\widehat{\mu}) = \widehat{\sigma}_{\widehat{\mu}}^2 = \frac{\widehat{\sigma}_{\widehat{\mu}}^2}{n} \qquad (2.26)$$

where σ^2 is the population variance and $\widehat{\sigma}^2$ is the sample variance.

Definition 2.2

The square root of the variance of the sample mean is called the **standard deviation of the sample mean**. It is also called the **standard error**.

Error

In statistics, error is the amount each data point misses the expected value or the average. To avoid using error for two different things, σ, or the standard deviation, is called the error and the $(X - \mu)^2 / N$ is called the variance or MSE. The term "MSE" is usually used in situations where part of the variation in data can be explained by trend line, treatment, block effect, and so forth, and the remaining unexplained portion is called MSE. The term "variance" is more commonly used for the population variance, when no portion of it could be explained by other factors.

The expected value is the parameter that represents the population. The actual observations deviate from their mean due to random error. The random error cannot be explained. In statistics, it is called the **error**. The error is the portion of the total variation that cannot be explained. The error is not necessarily a fixed amount. It is the amount not explained by the given tool. Change the tool and the error might change.

Some Algebraic Relations for Variance

Two important relations are used in dealing with variances and are worth reviewing.

1. The variance of a constant is zero.

$$\text{Var } (C) = 0 \tag{2.27}$$

2. The variance of a constant multiple of a variable is equal to the square of the constant times the variance.

$$\text{Var } (CX) = C^2 \text{ Var } (X) \tag{2.28}$$

Computational Formula (Short-Cut)

The definitional formula for variance may result in lots of rounding off, especially for a large population or sample, and cause an erroneous difference. If the mean is a never ending real number, the deviation will be a never ending real number. When this deviation is squared and added up, the small amount can add up and give a great bias. The computational formula(e) delay dividing the values as long as possible and do not introduce rounding off into the computation until the last stages.

The computational formula for the population variance is

$$\sigma^2 = \frac{\sum X^2 - \dfrac{(\sum X)^2}{N}}{N} \tag{2.29}$$

The derivation of the computational formula is relatively simple. It is important to point out that the letters X, N, and so on are dummy notation and are used to represent a variable. Sometimes other letters, such as Y and M, might be used instead. The concept is the same, only the notation is different. Therefore the variance can also be written as:

$$\sigma^2 = \frac{\sum Y^2 - \dfrac{(\sum Y)^2}{N}}{N} \tag{2.30}$$

Another computational formula delays division another step.

$$\sigma^2 = \frac{N \sum X^2 - (\sum X)^2}{N^2} \tag{2.31}$$

The derivation of this formula is no more difficult than the previous one. The corresponding computational formulas for the sample variance are:

$$\widehat{\sigma}^2 = \frac{\Sigma X^2 - \frac{(\Sigma X)^2}{n}}{n-1},$$ (2.32)

this is the more commonly used formula in most texts

or

$$\widehat{\sigma}^2 = \frac{n\Sigma X^2 - (\Sigma X)^2}{n(n-1)}$$ (2.33)

Example 2.15

Use the family income of gold miners from Example 2.1 and Example 2.3 to calculate the sample variance for the incomes of gold miners using the computational formula.

Income	X^2
66	4356
58	3364
71	5041
73	5329
64	4096
70	4900
66	4356
55	3025
75	5625
598	40092

Solution

$$\widehat{\sigma}^2 = \frac{\Sigma X^2 - \frac{(\Sigma X)^2}{n}}{n-1} = \frac{40092 - \frac{598^2}{9}}{8} = \frac{40092 - 39733.7778}{8}$$

$$= \frac{358.2222}{8} = 44.7777778$$

(Continued)

Or

$$\widehat{\sigma^2} = \frac{n \sum X^2 - (\sum X)^2}{n(n-1)} = \frac{9 \times 40092 - 357604}{9 \times 8} = 44.7777778$$

In this example the choice of the formula did not make any difference to the accuracy of the results.

Average of Several Variances

Sometimes it is important to average several variances. Suppose two or more samples are taken from the same population and estimated (sample) variances are obtained. In order to gain a better estimate of the population variance, all the variances should be averaged. If the sample sizes are the same, a simple average will provide the desired mean. If sample sizes are different, however, the observations, which in this case are the variances, should be weighted. The logical weight is the sample size, but since we are dealing with variances and unbiased estimates of population variance come from sample variance, which uses the degrees of freedom as the divisor, the weights to obtain the weighted mean of several sample variances are the degrees of freedom associated with each sample variance. This weighted mean of variances is usually called "pooled" variance. Recall that the formula for weighted mean is:

$$\mu = \frac{w_1 X_1 + w_2 X_2 + \cdots + w_N X_N}{w_1 + w_2 + \cdots + w_N} \tag{2.34}$$

Since we are dealing with the variances, and the customary name for the weighted average of variances is called "pooled variance," and since we use S^2 for sample variance we will use the commonly used symbol σ^2_{Pooled}. The weights $(w_1, w_2, \ldots, w_n)$ are degrees of freedom, and the Xs are sample variances, $\widehat{\sigma_1^2}, \widehat{\sigma_2^2}, \ldots \widehat{\sigma_n^2}$. Let $n_1, n_2, \ldots n_n$ be sample sizes. The formula for the case of two sample (estimated) variances is:

$$\widehat{\sigma^2_{Pooled}} = \frac{(n_1 - 1)\widehat{\sigma_1^2} + (n_2 - 1)\widehat{\sigma_2^2}}{(n_1 - 1) + (n_2 - 1)} \tag{2.35}$$

Repeat the pattern to average three or more sample variances.

Example 2.16

Calculate the weighted variance for the variances of the Microsoft stock prices between March 12 and March 30, 2010, and April 2 and April 21, 2012.

Solution

We already have the following results:

$$\widehat{\sigma_1^2} = 0.10941 \qquad \widehat{\sigma_2^2} = 0.372182$$

$$\sigma_{Pooled}^2 = \frac{(n_1 - 1)\widehat{\sigma_2^2} + (n_2 - 1)\widehat{\sigma_1^2}}{n_1 + n_2 - 2}$$

$$= \frac{(15 - 1)0.10941 + (15 - 1)0.372182}{15 + 15 - 2}$$

$$= \frac{1.5317 + 5.210554}{28} = 0.240798$$

In this and similar examples when the sample sizes are the same the use of weighted average and simple arithmetic average will be the same. Pooled variances are used in the test of hypothesis of equality of two means, as will be seen in Chapter 7.

Variance of Data with Frequency

Statistics is the science of summarizing information. This goal is achieved at several stages. The frequency distribution is a tabular summary of data. Often, the data are only available in frequency distribution format. In those cases it is desirable to be able to find the variance and other valuable parameters. The formula for the population variance for the frequency distribution is:

$$\sigma^2 = \frac{\Sigma f(X - \mu)^2}{\Sigma f} \tag{2.36}$$

The formula for the sample variance for the frequency distribution is:

$$\widehat{\sigma^2} = \frac{\Sigma f(X-\mu)^2}{\Sigma f - 1} \tag{2.37}$$

where f represents the frequency of each variable. The limits of Σ for population is N, while that of sample is n.

The computational formula for the population is:

$$\sigma^2 = \frac{\Sigma fX^2 - \dfrac{(\Sigma fX)^2}{\Sigma f}}{\Sigma f} \tag{2.38}$$

The computational formula for the sample is:

$$\widehat{\sigma^2} = \frac{\Sigma fX^2 - \dfrac{(\Sigma fX)^2}{\Sigma f}}{\Sigma f - 1} \tag{2.39}$$

Example 2.17

Use the family income of gold miners from Example 2.1 and Example2.3 that to calculate the sample variance for the first community using the frequency table.

$$66, 58, 71, 73, 64, 70, 66, 55, 75$$
$$65, 57, 71, 72, 63, 71, 65, 55, 71$$

Solution

Remember from Examples 2.1 and 2.7 the sample variance for these 18 men is equal to

$$\widehat{\sigma^2} = \frac{\Sigma(X - \widehat{\mu_X})^2}{n-1} = 42.68382$$

Suppose the raw data is presented in the frequency distribution form.

(*Continued*)

(*Continued*)

Observation	Frequency
55	2
57	1
58	1
63	1
64	1
65	2
66	2
70	1
71	4
72	1
73	1
75	1
Total	18

Note that there are 18 observations and not 12. The sample variance for the combined data is equal to 40.23529412. The calculation of the sample variance for the above data using the computational formula follows.

X	f	xf	X²	X²f
55	2	110	3025	6050
57	1	57	3249	3249
58	1	58	3364	3364
63	1	63	3969	3969
64	1	64	4096	4096
65	2	130	4225	8450
66	2	132	4356	8712
70	1	70	4900	4900
71	4	284	5041	20164
72	1	72	5184	5184
73	1	73	5329	5329
75	1	75	5625	5625
	18	1188		79092

$$\widehat{\sigma^2} = \frac{79092 - \dfrac{(1188)^2}{18}}{17} = \frac{79092 - 78408}{17} = \frac{684}{17} = 40.23529$$

The answer is the same as the one obtained using raw data. Therefore, summarizing the data into frequency distribution does not affect the **variance,** which will be addressed shortly. It does not affect the mean of the data arranged in a frequency distribution form either. The variance of the grouped data, however, will most likely be different than the actual variance. This is due partly to the fact that the class sizes are arbitrary, and mostly due to the formula.

Variance for Grouped Data

The formula for the variance of the grouped data for the population is:

$$\sigma^2 = \frac{\sum fM^2 - \frac{(\sum fM)^2}{\sum f}}{\sum f} \tag{2.40}$$

where M is the midpoint of each class. The formula for the variance of the grouped data for the sample is:

$$\widehat{\sigma^2} = \frac{\sum fM^2 - \frac{(\sum fM)^2}{\sum f}}{\sum f - 1} \tag{2.41}$$

where M is the midpoint of each class. The main difference between the two computational formulas is the denominator and the range of summation. The sum for the population covers the members of the population, N. The sum for the sample covers the members of the sample, n.

Measures of Associations

The measures of association determine the association between two variables or the degree of association between two variables.

Covariance

Population Covariance

The covariance is a measure of association between two variables. Let the variables be X and Y and their corresponding means be μ_X and μ_Y. The covariance is defined as:

$$\text{Cov}(X,Y) = \frac{\Sigma(X-\mu_X)(Y-\mu_Y)}{N} \qquad (2.42)$$

The covariance is the sum of the cross product of the deviations of the values of X and Y from their means divided by the population size. Sometimes it is written as σ_{XY} for the population covariance. This is not a standard deviation—it is the notation that reflects that the covariance has a sum of the cross products term. This compares to the notation of σ_X^2 for the variance of the population and σ_X for the standard deviation of the population.

The definitional formula for covariance suffers from the roundoff error and also can become very tedious if the means have long decimal places. The computational formula for covariance is:

$$\sigma_{XY} = \frac{\Sigma XY - \frac{(\Sigma X)(\Sigma Y)}{N}}{N} \qquad (2.43)$$

The derivation of the computational formula is not difficult.

Sample Covariance

In the sample covariance the population means are not known and have to be replaced by the sample means. Consequently the covariance loses a degree of freedom. The theoretical formula for the sample mean is:

$$\widehat{\sigma_{XY}} = \frac{\Sigma(X-\mu_X)(\widehat{X}-\widehat{\mu_Y})}{n-1} \qquad (2.44)$$

The computational formula for the sample covariance is:

$$\widehat{\sigma_{XY}} = \frac{\Sigma XY - \frac{(\Sigma X)(\Sigma Y)}{n}}{n-1} \qquad (2.45)$$

The derivation of Equation 2.45 is identical to the derivation of Equation 2.43. The covariance shows association between two variables. The magnitude of the covariance is a function of the degree of association as well as the units of measurement of the values. The size of covariance will change if the units of measurement are changed, for example from feet to inches or to yards.

Correlation Coefficient

The correlation coefficient ρ uses the measures of association and dispersion to provide a measure without a unit. The measure of association is the covariance and is placed on the numerator. The measures of dispersion are the standard deviation of the X and the standard deviation of the Y, which are placed in the denominator. All three are subject to change when the unit of measurement changes, but the correlation coefficient is immune.

$$\rho = \frac{\sigma_{XY}}{\sigma_X \sigma_Y} \qquad (2.46)$$

where σ_{XY} is the covariance, σ_X is the standard deviation of the X values, and σ_Y is the standard deviation of the Y values.

The sample correlation coefficient r is written as

$$\hat{\rho} = \frac{\widehat{\sigma_{XY}}}{\widehat{\sigma_X}\,\widehat{\sigma_Y}} \qquad (2.47)$$

Substituting the formulae for the population covariance and the standard deviations will yield:

$$\rho = \frac{\dfrac{\Sigma(X - \mu_X)(Y - \mu_Y)}{N}}{\sqrt{\dfrac{\Sigma(X - \mu_X)^2}{N}}\sqrt{\dfrac{\Sigma(Y - \mu_Y)^2}{N}}}, \qquad (2.48)$$

The corresponding formula for the sample correlation coefficient is:

$$\hat{\rho} = \frac{\dfrac{\Sigma(X - \widehat{\mu_X})(Y - \widehat{\mu_Y})}{n-1}}{\sqrt{\dfrac{\Sigma(X - \widehat{\mu_X})^2}{n-1}}\sqrt{\dfrac{\Sigma(Y - \widehat{\mu_Y})^2}{n-1}}} \qquad (2.49)$$

The corresponding computational form for the population and the sample are given in Equations 2.50 and 2.51 respectively.

$$\rho = \frac{\sum XY - \dfrac{(\sum X)(\sum Y)}{N}}{\sqrt{\sum X^2 - \dfrac{(\sum X)^2}{N}}\sqrt{\sum Y^2 - \dfrac{(\sum Y)^2}{N}}} \tag{2.50}$$

$$= \frac{\dfrac{\sum XY - \dfrac{(\sum X)(\sum Y)}{n}}{n-1}}{\sqrt{\sum X^2 - \dfrac{(\sum X)^2}{n}}\sqrt{\sum Y^2 - \dfrac{(\sum Y)^2}{n}}} \tag{2.51}$$

Notice that the only difference between the population and the sample correlation coefficient in the computation formulas is the use of N instead of n. Each is the size of its corresponding data. The difference is conceptual and reflects their origin. Do not overlook the fact that ρ is a parameter and a constant, while r is the statistics and a variable. The sample correlation coefficient r is used to estimate and draw inference about the population correlation coefficient ρ.

CHAPTER 3

Some Applications of Descriptive Statistics

Introduction

The descriptive statistics that were covered in Chapters 1 and 2 provide summary statistics and graphical methods to present data in a more concise and meaningful way. Although those measures and methods are useful in their own right as demonstrated in the previous chapters, they are also used to further create more powerful statistical measures: some of which are discussed in this chapter. Later, in Chapter 7, these measures are utilized to provide statistical inference, which is the foundation for testing hypotheses in every branch of science.

Coefficient of Variation

The coefficient of variation is the ratio of the standard deviation to the mean. In other words, the coefficient of variation expresses the standard deviation (the average error) as a percentage of the average of the population or sample. It is a relative measure of dispersion. It measures the standard deviation in terms of the mean.

$$CV = \frac{\sigma}{\mu} \tag{3.1}$$

The coefficient of variation is independent of the units of measurement of the variables. If two populations have the same standard deviation, the one with the lower coefficient of variation has less variation.

Example 3.1

The manager of the mortgage department in a local bank has gathered the amounts for approved second mortgage loans for every 100th customer. The amounts are in dollars.

5,672	6,578	9,700	12,000	9,000	6,350
4,495	6,900	7,835	8,750	10,000	12,000
6,500	7,200	8,000	18,000	19,000	12,000
4,560	1,500	5,900	5,450	6,500	1,800
1,900	10,500				

Calculate the coefficient of variation.

Solution

$$CV = \frac{\sigma}{\mu} = \frac{4257.58}{8003.46} = 0.532$$

Coefficient of variation represents the average error as a fraction of the expected value. The coefficient of variation is useful in comparing data with different magnitudes. Assume that two stocks are rated similarly where they have the same characteristics such as objectives and the amount and frequency of dividends. In order to compare the **relative variability** of the average price of the two stocks, we use the coefficient of variation. Relative to the mean price, the stock with the lower coefficient of variation indicates lower variation and hence lower risk.

The coefficient of variation is also useful in the comparison of unrelated data, especially when the unit of measurement is different. For example, if the efficiency of a gas-powered lawn mower is compared to the reliability of an electric edger, then the machine with the lower coefficient of variation is more reliable.

The most effective use of the coefficient of variation is in the comparison of two different experiments by finding the ratios of their respective coefficients of variation, as is seen in the following example.

Example 3.2

Refer to the stock prices for Wal-Mart and Microsoft from Example 2.2. Determine which one is riskier using the data for March 2012.

Table 3.1. Closing Prices of Wal-Mart (WMT) and Microsoft (MSFT) for the period from March 12 to March 30 and from April 2 to April 21, 2012

Date	WMT	MSFT	Date	WMT	MSFT
12 Mar.	$60.68	$32.04	2 Apr.	$61.36	$32.29
13 Mar.	$61.00	$32.67	3 Apr.	$60.65	$31.94
14 Mar.	$61.08	$32.77	4 Apr.	$60.26	$31.21
15 Mar.	$61.23	$32.85	5 Apr.	$60.67	$31.52
16 Mar.	$60.84	$32.60	9 Apr.	$60.13	$31.10
19 Mar.	$60.74	$32.20	10 Apr.	$59.93	$30.47
20 Mar.	$60.60	$31.99	11 Apr.	$59.80	$30.35
21 Mar.	$60.56	$31.91	12 Apr.	$60.14	$30.98
22 Mar.	$60.65	$32.00	13 Apr.	$59.77	$30.81
23 Mar.	$60.75	$32.01	16 Apr.	$60.58	$31.08
26 Mar.	$61.20	$32.59	17 Apr.	$61.87	$31.44
27 Mar.	$61.09	$32.52	18 Apr.	$62.06	$31.14
28 Mar.	$61.19	$32.19	19 Apr.	$61.75	$31.01
29 Mar.	$60.82	$32.12	20 Apr.	$62.45	$32.42
30 Mar.	$61.20	$32.26	21 Apr.	$59.54	$32.12

Solution

Let's refer to Wal-Mart stock as "1" and to the Microsoft stock as "2." Recall that we calculated the means and standard deviations for these stocks. The following information is available for the two stocks. Which one is relatively less risky and thus better?

$$\widehat{\mu_1} = 60.91 \qquad \widehat{\sigma_1} = 0.2428$$

$$\widehat{\mu_2} = 32.31 \qquad \widehat{\sigma_2} = 0.3191$$

$$CV_1 = \frac{0.2428}{60.91} = 0.0040$$

(*Continued*)

(*Continued*)

$$CV_2 = \frac{0.3191}{32.31} = 0.0099$$

$$\frac{CV_1}{CV_2} = \frac{0.0040}{0.0099} = 0.4$$

Therefore, stock 1, Wal-Mart, is less risky than stock 2, Microsoft.

Z Score

The Z score is a useful and intuitive concept and, as it will become evident, is used often in statistics. The Z score uses two of the more common parameters, the mean and the standard deviation. The problem of accurate and consistent measurement has been a difficult subject throughout history. The yardstick differed from one time to another and across different locations and cultures. Different countries and rulers tried to unify the unit of measurement. The closest unit to become universally accepted is the meter. Even the metric system is not commonly used in all quarters in spite of its ease and applicability. The metric system has its limitations too. One problem is the difference in scale. The following example demonstrates the problem.

County fairs have farming contests and they give prizes for the "best" in different categories. For example, the farmer with the biggest produce receives a prize. But by nature, even the largest apple on record is not a match for any pumpkin. Would it be fair to compare the amount of a cow's milk with that of a goat? In economic terms, how can we compare the output of the most productive small manufacturer to that of a larger one, which is fully automated?

In statistics, everything is measured in relative terms. It makes no sense to compare the weight of a peach to that of a pumpkin, but comparing their relative weights makes perfect sense. Let's have a peach that weighs 8.4 ounces and a pumpkin that weighs 274.9 ounces. Although the pumpkin is actually heavier, that might not be the case when other factors are considered. One factor is the average weight of peaches and pumpkins. A typical peach is about 6 ounces, while a typical pumpkin is 22 pounds, or 352 ounces. The peach in this example is somewhat heavier than an average peach while the pumpkin is actually lighter than an average pumpkin. Therefore, relatively speaking, the peach is heavier than the pumpkin. However, this is not enough. We also need to divide the distance from the mean for each produce by its typical or average error. Let's assume that the standard deviation for peaches is 1.15 ounces. Therefore, the amount that the peach exceeds its average as measured by its own yardstick is $(8.4 - 6) / 1.15 = 2.086$ standard deviation. Let's assume that the standard deviation for the pumpkin is 2.57 pounds or $16 \times 2.57 = 41.12$ ounces. Therefore, the pumpkin is $(274.9 - 352) / 41.12 = -1.875$ standard deviations below its expected weight. Therefore, the pumpkin is actually sub-par, while the peach is a prize winner. This is the essence of what is called a **Z score** and the procedure is known as **standardization**.

The Z score is defined as follows:

$$Z = \frac{\text{Observed} - \text{Expected}}{\text{Standard Deviation of the Observed}} \qquad (3.2)$$

$$Z = \frac{X - \mu}{\sigma} \qquad (3.3)$$

The expected value of an observation is its mean or (μ), its standard deviation is (σ). To obtain the Z score of an observed value, subtract its mean from its observed value and divide the result by the standard deviation of the observation.

The distance of an observation from its expected value is also called its **error**. Some of the different aspects of error will be discussed later in this chapter. The Z score is a scaled error. The unit of measurement of Z score is the standard deviation of the population or its sample estimate. Obtaining the Z score of an observation is also known as standardizing the value. The standardization process can be applied to any data or observation. If the item under consideration is a single observation from the population, the result is called the **Z score**.

$$Z = \frac{X - \mu}{\sigma}$$

Suppose two students are given the task of measuring the error of an observation. The first student found that the observation is 41.6666 feet. In fact, the decimal place is never-ending. Disliking decimal places and especially the never-ending ones, he measured the deviation of the data point from the mean in inches and was relieved to find out that it has no decimal place. He presented his error of the observation as 500 inches. The second student, using an electronic measuring "tape," subtracted the observation from the mean and reported 0.007891414 miles as the error. While the first error seems large and the second seems small, both are the same. Note that 500 inches is 41.6666667 feet or 0.007891414 miles. Z score provides a unique and comparable measure of error to avoid the confusion that may arise from changes in units of measurement. Every error is reported in the units of its own standard deviation. Since the Z score is reported in terms of the standard deviation, it allows comparison of unrelated data measured in different units.

Z Score for a Sample Mean

If the value under consideration is the sample mean, $\hat{\mu}$, the resulting Z score would be:

$$Z = \frac{\hat{\mu} - \mu}{\sigma_{\hat{\mu}}} \qquad (3.4)$$

where $\hat{\mu}$ is the sample mean, μ is its expected value, which is also the population mean, and the standard deviation of the sample is $\sigma_{\hat{\mu}} = \sigma/\sqrt{n}$. The standard deviation of the sample mean is also known as the **standard error**. In order to calculate the Z score for a sample mean, it is necessary to know the population variance. Usually, we do not know the population variance either. When the population variance is unknown, we must use a t value instead. We will discuss t distribution in more detail in Chapter 4. For the time being, we will assume that we know the population variance. The most realistic assumption is to use the sample variance as if it were the population variance.

Theorem 3.1 Chebyshev Theorem

The proportion of observations falling within k standard deviations of the mean is **at least**

$$\left(1 - \frac{1}{K^2}\right). \tag{3.5}$$

This is the same **Z score** concept. The theorem indicates that we need to find the difference of a value from its mean, that is, $(X - \mu)$. Since the theorem applies to all the values within k standard deviations, that is, $k\sigma$ on either side of the mean, the absolute value is desired. The theorem sets a minimum limit for the $|X - \mu| < k\sigma$. Therefore, the Chebyshev theorem states that:

$$P\left(|X - \mu| < k\sigma\right) \geq \left(1 - \frac{1}{K^2}\right) \tag{3.6}$$

But since σ is a non-negative value, dividing both sides of the inequality $|X - \mu| < k\sigma$ by σ will not change the sign. Therefore,

$$P\left(\frac{|X - \mu|}{\sigma} < k\right) \geq \left(1 - \frac{1}{K^2}\right)$$

$$P\left(|Z| < k\right) \geq \left(1 - \frac{1}{K^2}\right) \tag{3.7}$$

As is evident, the Z score is the core of the Chebyshev theorem. Chebyshev was one of the major contributors to the Central Limit Theorem, which will be discussed in Chapter 5.

The first part of the equation $\{P(|Z| < k)\}$ is the same as the **confidence interval** of a range, which is covered in Chapter 6. The concept of Z score is also used in statistical inference, which is covered in Chapter 7.

Example 3.3

Determine what percentage of the Microsoft stock prices from March 12 to March 30, 2012, lay within the two standard deviations of their mean. Verify the correctness of the result by counting the prices that are within two standard deviations of the mean. Assume the population's mean and variance are the same as the sample mean and variance, respectively. See Example 3.2 for data.

Solution

The sample mean and sample variance are given in Example 3.2 as:

$$\mu = \widehat{\mu_2} = 32.31 \qquad \sigma = \widehat{\sigma_2} = 0.3191$$

Note that we are using the notation for population mean and population standard deviation to make sure that the theorem applies. The theorem requires the knowledge of population mean and standard deviation, and we are assuming them to be the values we obtained from the sample.

Insert the data in Equation 3.6:

$$P\left(|X - \mu| < k\sigma\right) \geq \left(1 - \frac{1}{K^2}\right)$$

$$P(|X - 32.31| < 2\,(0.3191)) \geq \left(1 - \frac{1}{4}\right)$$

$$P(|X - 32.31| < 0.6382) \geq 0.75$$

Therefore, at least 75% of the 15 observations will be within two standard deviations of the mean. Next we calculate the range "within 2 standard deviations."

$$32.31 - 0.6382 = \$31.67$$
$$32.31 + 0.6382 = \$32.95$$

The easiest way to verify that the result is valid is to sort the data. You will notice that the lowest price is $31.91 and the highest price is $32.85. Therefore, 100% of the data are within two standard deviations of the mean, which exceeds the predicted minimal percentage of 75%.

Standardization

In order to be able to compare different objects with different scales we need a tool that places everything in a unified perspective. A value can be **standardized** by finding its distance from the population mean, that is, its **individual error**, and then scale the result or put it in perspective with respect to its standard deviation.

$$Z = \frac{\text{Observed} - \text{Expected}}{\text{Standard Deviation of the Observed}} \tag{3.8}$$

The unit of measurement is in standard deviation.

If a data point is 72 and its expected value and standard deviation are 70 and 4.3, respectively, then the estimated error is $\hat{\epsilon} = 72 - 70 = 2$. Its standardized value is:

$$\text{Standardized value} = \frac{2}{4.3} = 0.465$$

The data point is said to be 0.465 standard deviations to the right of its mean. If an ordinary data point is selected and its standardized value is calculated, then that value is called a Z score.

$$Z = \frac{X - \mu}{\sigma} \tag{3.9}$$

Therefore, the two statements "the data point is 0.465 standard deviations above its mean" and "the Z score for the data point is 0.465" mean the same. Had the Z score been negative, then the data point would have been on the left side of its mean. If a random variable is from a population with known mean and variance, then its standardized value is called a Z score.

Example 3.4

Calculate the Z scores for closing prices of Microsoft stock from March 12 to March 30. Assume that the population's mean and variance are equal to the sample mean and variance, respectively.

(Continued)

(*Continued*)

Solution

Use Equation 3.9 and the following values from Example 3.2:

$$\mu = \widehat{\mu_2} = 32.31 \qquad \sigma = \widehat{\sigma_2} = 0.3191$$

Note that we are using the notation for population mean and population standard deviation to make sure that the theorem applies. The theorem requires the knowledge of population mean and standard deviation, and we are assuming that we know them to be the values we obtained from the sample.

Date	MSFT	Z Score
12 Mar.	$32.04	−0.86
13 Mar.	$32.67	1.11
14 Mar.	$32.77	1.43
15 Mar.	$32.85	1.68
16 Mar.	$32.60	0.89
19 Mar.	$32.20	−0.36
20 Mar.	$31.99	−1.02
21 Mar.	$31.91	−1.27
22 Mar.	$32.00	−0.99
23 Mar.	$32.01	−0.95
26 Mar.	$32.59	0.86
27 Mar.	$32.52	0.64
28 Mar.	$32.19	−0.39
29 Mar.	$32.12	−0.61
30 Mar.	$32.26	−0.17
		0.00

The sum of the Z scores is provided at the bottom, which is zero. This is a mathematical property of **individual errors**, which add up to zero. See Definition 3.5.

Correlation Coefficient Is the Average of the Product of Z Scores

Correlation coefficient was introduced in Chapter 2. It measures the degree of association between two variables.

$$\rho = \frac{\sigma_{XY}}{\sigma_X \sigma_Y} = \frac{\frac{\Sigma(X - \mu_X)(Y - \mu_Y)}{N}}{\sigma_X \sigma_Y} = \frac{\Sigma\left(\frac{(X - \mu_X)}{\sigma_X} \times \frac{(Y - \mu_Y)}{\sigma_Y}\right)}{N} = \frac{\Sigma Z_X Z_Y}{N}$$

The above derivation depends on the definition of a parameter as a constant. This allows moving parameters, such as standard deviations, into a summation notation. Note that anything that is added and divided by the number of observations is an average number. In this case, the product of two Z scores $(Z_X Z_Y)$ is added and divided by N. Hence, correlation coefficient is the average of the product of two Z scores.

Standard Error

When data is obtained from a sample, the standard deviation of the estimated sample statistics is called a **standard error**. This concept will be addressed in detail when the sampling distribution of the sample mean is discussed in Chapter 5. As the distributional properties of **sample standard deviation** are different than that of the **population standard deviation**, we had to assume that the standard deviation obtained from the samples in Examples 3.2 and 3.4 were known to be the same as the population standard deviation.

$$\text{Standard Error} = \sigma_{\hat{\mu}} = \sqrt{\sigma_{\hat{\mu}}^2}$$

Usually, the standard deviation of the sample mean is also **unknown** and has to be estimated, which is represented with a **hat**.

$$\text{Sample Standard Error} = \widehat{\sigma_{\hat{\mu}}} = \sqrt{\widehat{\sigma_{\hat{\mu}}^2}}$$

Therefore, the correct representation of the t statistics from a sample is:

$$t = \frac{\hat{\mu} - \mu}{\sigma_{\hat{\mu}}}$$

(3.10)

Note that Equation 3.10 is called a t and not a Z as in Equation 3.4. The reason for the difference in names is due to the difference in the denominators of the two equations. Gosset[1] showed that if the population variance is unknown and has to be estimated by the sample variance, then the resulting standardization does not have a normal distribution and does in fact have a **student t distribution**.

Definition 3.1

The Degree of Freedom is the number of elements that can be chosen freely in a sample. The degree of freedom only applies to a sample. The population parameters are constant values and are estimated by sample statistics.

Example 3.5

Let us have a small population, say, sized five. For example, consider a family with five children of ages 3, 5, 7, 8, and 9. Let us take samples without replacement of size three from this population. There will be 10 different possible samples. The population mean is 32/5 = 6.4, that is, the average age of the children is 6.4 years. The **mean** value governs the outcome of the average of the mean of the samples, as is demonstrated below. The 10 possible samples and their corresponding means are:

Sample	Mean
8, 3, 7	6
8, 3, 5	5.333
8, 3, 9	6.667
8, 7, 5	6.667
8, 7, 9	8
8, 5, 9	7.333
3, 7, 5	5
3, 7, 9	6.333
3, 5, 9	5.667
7. 5. 9	7
Total	64

(*Continued*)

Even though none of the sample means equals the population mean, the population mean has exerted its influence on the sample means. Find the average of the 10 possible sample means. It is 64 / 10 = 6.4. Therefore, the expected value or the average of all the possible sample means is equal to the population mean. Even if we do not know the population mean, every population has a mean, and that mean will influence all the sample means. It is even possible to prove, mathematically, that the average of sample means is equal to the population mean. In mathematical statistics the average is formally defined as the **expected value** and is represented by an E, therefore, E $(\hat{\mu}) = \mu$.

In the Example 3.5, this means that any 9 of these 10 possible samples can be **chosen freely**. After 9 samples and their means are obtained, the 10th, or the last one, is forced to have a mean value such that the average of all the sample means equals the population mean. Let us assume that the fourth possible sample in the above list is the one that is not taken yet, and its mean has not been calculated. The mean of this sample has to be 64 − 57.222 = 6.778. Within this sample any two numbers can be selected at random, but the last one must be such a number that its average equals 6.778. Two of the three numbers 8, 7, and 5 can be randomly selected. Say 5 and 7 are selected. The last number must be 8, since this is the only number that will make the average of this sample equal to 6.778 and the average of all the sample means equal to $\mu = 6.4$. In general, **n − 1** sample points can be selected at random, but the value of the remaining one will be determined automatically by the value of the population. One degree of freedom is lost for every parameter that is unknown and must be estimated by a statistics.

Computation of variance requires the knowledge of the population mean.

$$\sigma^2 = \frac{\Sigma(X - \mu)^2}{N}$$

If the population mean μ is not known, the value of σ^2 cannot be determined. If instead of μ its estimate is obtained, then the sample mean, or $\hat{\mu}$ is used. The sample variance then is:

$$\widehat{\sigma^2} = \frac{\Sigma(X - \hat{\mu})^2}{n - 1}$$

and it will lose one degree of freedom. The result of the adjustment to the sample variance—that is, dividing by the **degree of freedom**, $n - 1$, instead of the sample size, n—is that the sample variance becomes an **unbiased estimate** of the population variance.[2]

Properties of Estimators

Sample statistics are used as estimators of the population parameters. Since sample statistics provide a single value, they are also called **point estimates**. It is desirable to be able to compare different point estimates of the same parameters and provide useful properties.

Let θ, pronounced **theta**, be the population parameter of interest. Let its estimate be $\hat{\theta}$, pronounced **theta hat**. Like any other point estimate, $\hat{\theta}$ is a sample statistic and a known variable.

Definition 3.2   definition of unbiased

If the expected value of a point estimate equals the population parameter, then the estimate is unbiased. In symbols:

$$E(\hat{\theta}) = \theta \tag{3.11}$$

It can be shown that the sample **mean** ($\hat{\mu}$), **variance** ($\widehat{\sigma^2}$), and **proportion** ($\hat{\pi}$) are all unbiased estimates of their corresponding population parameters.

$$E(\hat{\mu}) = \mu$$

$$E(\widehat{\sigma^2}) = \sigma^2$$

$$E(\hat{\pi}) = \pi$$

Definition 3.3

The **efficiency** of a point estimator is said to be higher if it has a smaller variance. If $\hat{\theta}_1$ and $\hat{\theta}_2$ are two point estimates of θ and Var $(\hat{\theta}_1)$ < Var $(\hat{\theta}_2)$ then $\hat{\theta}_1$ is more efficient than $\hat{\theta}_2$. For example, the sample mean is more efficient than the sample median in estimating the population mean.

Definition 3.4

A point estimate is a **consistent** estimator if its variance gets smaller as the sample size increases. The variance of the sample mean

$$\widehat{\sigma^2} = \frac{\sigma^2}{n}$$

will decrease as the sample size increases. As the sample size increases, the sample mean will have a smaller and smaller variance. And as it is an unbiased estimate of the population mean, it will get closer and closer to the population mean.

Error

Statistics deals with random phenomena. For a set of values $X_1, X_2, ..., X_n$ there is a representative or expected value (mean). The Greek letter μ is used to represent the expected value. The difference of each value from the expected value, also called the deviation from the mean, represents an **individual error**.

Definition 3.5

An **individual error** is the difference between the value of an observation and its expected value. The **expected value** or the **mean** is the best estimate or representative of a population and, hence, the sample. For example, the average starting salary for an economics major in 2011 was $54,400. If a recent economics graduate is selected at random his or her expected income is $54,000 then the error associated with this observation is $400. In other words, the observation missed the expected value by $400. The reason for calling the deviation an error is that we do not have any explanation for the deviation other than a random error. Therefore, the **error** is what we cannot explain. Since observations vary at random, the errors vary at random as well. Furthermore, the portion that cannot be explained depends on the model or procedure used. Sometimes it is possible to explain part of variation of observations from their expected value by developing more sophisticated methods. The portions that can be explained by the new procedure are no longer "unexplained," and, thus, not part of the error any more. The unexplainable portion is still called an error. Note that unless all the observations in a sample or population are identical, they will deviate from their expected value and, hence, have a random error.

Since there are as many individual errors as there are observations, we need to summarize them into fewer variables. A popular and useful statistic is the average or the mean. However, the average of individual errors is always zero because the sum of all errors is zero. Recall that individual errors are deviations from their expected values, some of which are negative and the others are positive. Thus, by definition, they cancel each other out and the sum of all deviations is always zero. Symmetric distributions have equal numbers of positive and negative individual errors, but this is not a necessary condition for their sum to add to zero. The sum of individual errors for non-symmetric distributions is also zero, in spite of the fact that the count of negative values is different from the count of the positive values. This is due to the fact that the expected value or the mean is the same as the **center of gravity** of the data. Imagine data on a line where they are arranged from smallest to largest. Placing a pin at the point of the average will balance the line.

There are several ways to overcome individual errors canceling each other out. One way is to use the absolute value of the individual errors. The average of the absolute values of the individual errors is called **mean absolute error (MAE)**. The mean absolute error is commonly used in time series analysis. One advantage of MAE is that it has the same unit of measurement as the actual observations.

Another way to prevent individual errors from canceling each other out is to square them before averaging them. We are already familiar with this concept, which is called a **variance**.

Definition 3.6

The **variance** is the average of the sum of the squared individual errors.

One advantage of variance over the mean absolute error is that it squares errors, which gives more power to values that are further away from the expected value. This makes the variances disproportionately large as individual errors get larger. The variances use of the squared values of the individual errors is its shortcoming as well because the unit of measurement for the variance is the square of the unit of measurement of the observations. If the observations are about length in feet, then the variance will be in feet squared, which is the unit of measurement of an area and not length. Seldom, if ever, the squared values of economic phenomenon have any meaning. If the variable of interest is price, measured in dollars, then the unit of measurement of its variance is in dollars-squared, which has no economic meaning. To remedy this problem, it is necessary to take the square root of variance.

Definition 3.7

The **standard deviation** is the square root of the variance.

Definition 3.8

The **standard deviation** is the **average error**.

How Close Is Close Enough?

If the sum of the residual is not zero, then check your formulas and computations. If the definitional formulas are used or the results are rounded off at early stages, the sum of individual errors may be different than zero. Use of computational formulas and less round-off will reduce or eliminate this problem provided the sample size is sufficiently large. If you use five decimal places, the final result can be accurate to about four decimal places. If you have been using five decimal places in your calculations and the sum of the residual is 0.00007, the property has not been violated. It is zero to four decimal places as expected.

Sum of Squares

The sum of squares of deviation of values from their expected value (mean) is a prominent component of statistics. As we saw previously, the square of these individual errors divided by the population size is called population variance. The concept is the same for a sample, except that the divisor is the degree of freedom. Earlier, it was explained that the portion of the phenomenon that cannot be explained is called an error, and that the variance is one way of representing it. When alternative models are used to explain part of the error, it is more meaningful to focus on the numerator alone, at least at first. The numerator, or variance, is also called **total sum of squares (TSS)**. Once a set of data is collected then the TSS becomes fixed and will not change. The TSS will only change if another sample from the same population was collected at random. Decomposition of TSS is very common in a branch of statistics called **experimental design**. In experimental design methodology TSS is decomposed into different components based on the design. These components include treatment SS, block SS, main effect SS, and so forth. In all cases there is always a component that remains unexplained, and is referred to as residual or error SS. By definition, dividing this unexplained remainder by appropriate degrees of freedom would result in the variance of the experiment, customarily known as **mean squared error (MSE)** or mean squares error. As one would expect, the square root of MSE is called **root MSE**, which is the same as the **standard error**. Just as a reminder:

$$\text{MSE} = \frac{\text{sum(observed} - \text{expected})^2}{n - k}$$

Note that the term in the parentheses is the individual error. The k in the denominator is the number of parameters in the model, and the entire denominator is the degrees of freedom.

Skewness

As you noticed in Chapter 2, several of the relationships between mean, mode, and median were described. The relationship between these parameters can also be used to determine if the data are symmetric and the extent of the pointedness of the data. Of course, the data cannot be flat, pointed, symmetric, or skewed. The fact is that we are talking about the shapes of data when they are plotted.

Definition 3.9

The **skewness** refers to the extent that a graph of a distribution function deviates from symmetry. A distribution function that is not symmetric is either negatively skewed, as in Figure 3.1, or positively skewed, as in Figure 3.2.

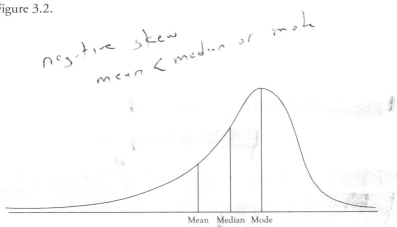

Figure 3.1. Negatively skewed distribution.

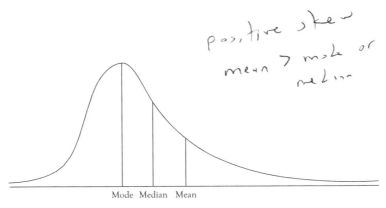

Figure 3.2. Positively skewed distribution.

Relation Between Mean, Median, and Mode

The mean, median, and mode of symmetrical distributions are identical. If the distribution is positively skewed, the order of magnitude is

$$\text{Mode} < \text{Median} < \text{Mean} \qquad (3.12)$$

If the distribution is negatively skewed, the order of magnitude is

$$\text{Mean} < \text{Median} < \text{Mode} \qquad (3.13)$$

The importance of skewness is in its use to test if the data follows a normal distribution. Normal distribution function is discussed in Chapter 4.

Definition 3.10

The Pearson coefficient of **skewness** is defined as:

$$S = \frac{3(\text{mean} - \text{median})}{\text{standard deviation}}$$

The range of skewness is $-3 < S < 3$, and for a symmetric distribution $S = 0$. The sign of the Pearson coefficient of skewness determines if it is positively or negatively skewed.

Definition 3.11

Kurtosis is a measure of pointedness or flatness of a symmetric distribution. The exact definition of Kurtosis requires the knowledge of the moments, which is beyond the scope of this text. A positive Kurtosis indicates the distribution is more pointed than the normal distribution, and a negative value for Kurtosis indicates the distribution is flatter than normal distribution. Kurtosis and skewness are commonly used to test whether a data set follows a normal distribution.

CHAPTER 4

Distribution Functions

Definitions and Some Concepts

Sometimes it is possible to represent random variables as a function in a way that the function can determine the probability of an outcome of the random variable.

Definition 4.1

The outcome of a **random variable** is determined by chance. The outcome of a random variable might be constant as in the case of observing a head when a coin is flipped, or it can be a variable value such as the length of time it takes for different students to learn this chapter. The subject "statistics" is used to study the properties of random variables and how they behave.

Definition 4.2

The **probability distribution** determines the probability of the outcomes of a random variable. In its simplest form, the probability distribution consists of values and probabilities. The probability distribution for flipping a coin is:

$$f(x) = \begin{cases} \text{Head with probability } 1/2 \\ \text{Tail with probability } 1/2 \end{cases}$$

There are more formal ways to define probability distribution that are beyond the scope of this text. A distribution function can be presented in the form of a function, a table, or a statement. The subject of probability distribution is vast, but we will focus on the few items needed to continue our discussion. There are two types of random variables, **discrete** and **continuous**.

Definition 4.3

A **discrete random** variable consists of integers only.

Definition 4.4

A **continuous random** variable can take any value over a range.

Definition 4.5

The **probability distribution for a discrete random** variable is called a discrete probability distribution and is represented as $f(x)$.

Definition 4.6

The **probability distribution for a continuous random** variable is called a probability density function.

In this text we may use distribution function for both discrete and continuous random variable as a matter of convenience.

Continuous Distribution Functions

There are numerous distribution functions, both discrete and continuous. In this text, for the sake of space only, the distribution functions that are used to provide inference are discussed.

Normal Distribution Function

Normal distribution functions are the most important and most widely used distribution function. Standardized normal distribution functions, called standard normal, can be applied in any area and situation, provided that one is assured of the normality and either knows, or can estimate, the mean and variance of the distribution. Standard normal values are the Z scores of values that have a normal distribution. Converting values from different normal distributions with different means and variances to standard normal allows us to compare them. Furthermore, any standardized value can be compared with the theoretical standard normal table.

Since normal distribution is a continuous distribution function, and there are infinitely many points on any continuous interval, the probability of any single point is always zero. For continuous distribution functions, such as normal distribution, the probability is calculated for an interval. Direct computation of such probabilities requires integral calculus. For simplicity, a table of standard normal values is used. Spreadsheets such as Microsoft Excel are capable of computing the standard normal values. A table of values for normal distribution is provided in the Appendix.

Properties of Normal Distribution

A normal distribution is depicted in Figure 4.1. The normal distribution curve is unimodal and symmetric. Consequently, its mean, mode, and median are all the same and fall in the middle of the curve. You may notice that the tails of the normal curve do not touch the x-axis. This is another property of the normal distribution. The x-axis is actually an asymptote of the functions, which means the curve does not touch the axis even at infinity. This implies that the tails are stretched to infinity, but in practice, we do not stretch the tails that far. As you will soon see, the probability of the tail areas becomes very negligible not too far from the center, making it unnecessary to be concerned with infinity. A normal distribution has two parameters: its mean and variance. In other words, the mean and variance of a normal distribution determine its specific center and spread. Since distribution is commonly used and has so many applications, it has become known as normal distribution. Furthermore, the mean and variance of the normal distribution are represented by μ and σ^2, respectively.

The area under the normal curve is equal to 1, as is the area under any distribution density function. Customarily, the distance from the center of normal distribution is measured by its standard deviation. If two

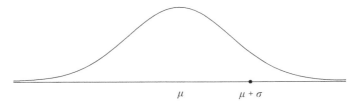

Figure 4.1. Normal distribution with mean = μ and variance = σ^2.

normal distribution functions have the same mean and variance then the area under the curve for two points that are the same distance from the center are equal. By converting any normal distribution to one with a mean of 0 and a standard deviation of 1, we are able to calculate the area under the curve between the center and any point for any normal distribution regardless of its mean and variance. The area under normal distribution represents the probability between any two points on the curve. We will soon see that the probability for a point to be within one standard deviation from the mean of a normal distribution function is about 68%. Since the normal distribution is symmetric, it is possible to calculate area from the center to a point on one side of the center, and the probability for a point of the same distance from the mean on the other side, which will be equal.

Standardizing Values from a Normal Distribution

In Chapter 3 we discussed Z score, which can be used to compare dissimilar things by converting them to the same basis, which is by obtaining their deviations from their expected values and scaling them by their standard deviation. The process is also called **standardization**. Standardized values are comparable. The same is true if we standardize the values of a normal distribution. Note that the mean of normal distribution is μ and its variance is σ^2. As a result of standardization of a normal distribution, one obtains a normal distribution for which the mean is 0 and the variance is 1. We show this as $N(0, 1)$. Since the area under any normal distribution is equal to 1 regardless of the value of its mean or variance, the area under $N(0, 1)$ is also equal to 1. This makes it possible to create a single table for $N(0, 1)$ and generalize to any other normal distributions with different means and variances. The graph for $N(0, 1)$ is exactly the same as the graph in Figure 4.1. The one depicted below in Figure 4.2 has

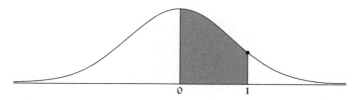

Figure 4.2. The area under the normal distribution between 0 and 1.

the added feature that marks the point which is one standard deviation to the right of the center.

Area Under a Normal Distribution with Mean Zero and Variance One

To calculate area under a normal distribution, we can use Table A1 from the Appendix. This table is similar to most other normal tables except it is more accurate because it graduates at half of the customary steps of most normal tables. To read the value of 1.0, go to the left margin of the table and identify the row marked 1.0. Then identify the column marked 0. The value at their intersection is 0.3413, which is the probability corresponding to the shaded area between 0, the mean, and point 1, which is one standard deviation away from the mean to the right.

In the above section we stated that about 68%, or a little more than 2/3 of all observations, are within one standard deviation of the center. Since the points on each side of the center are the mirror images of each other, the probability of being one standard deviation below the mean is the same as the probability of being one standard deviation above the mean, and hence equal to 0.3413. Therefore, the probability of being within one standard deviation of the mean is double the amount of 0.6826, or about 68%. Computations of other values are similar.

$$P\ (0 < Z < 1.49) = 0.4319$$
$$P\ (0 < Z < 2.63) = 0.4957$$
$$P\ (-1.52 < Z < 0) = 0.4357$$

For other variations, it is best to graph the area and perform simple algebra to obtain the results.

$$P\ (-1.52 < Z < 1.49) = P\ (-1.52 < Z < 0) + P\ (0 < Z < 1.49)$$
$$= 0.4357 + 0.4319 = 0.8676$$

See Figure 4.3 for clarification.

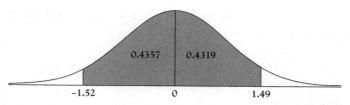

Figure 4.3. Area under normal distribution between −1.52 and 1.49.

$$P \ (-1.52 < Z < -1.49) = P \ (-1.52 < Z < 0) + P \ (-1.49 < Z < 0)$$
$$= 0.4357 - 0.4319 = 0.0038$$

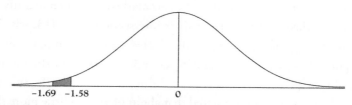

Figure 4.4. Area under normal distribution between −1.69 and −1.58.

See Figure 4.4 for finding the shaded area for the last example. Make sure you put the point further away from the center first, because of rules of geometry, and this will guarantee that you would not obtain a negative probability, which does not make any sense.

Obtaining Probability Values for Normal Distribution with Excel

The above examples can be obtained by using the following command in Excel.

$$=NORMDIST(1.49,0,1,1) - 0.5 = 0.43188$$

The formula consists of:

$$=NORMDIST(X, \text{mean, standard deviation, True})$$

where "true" represents the "cumulative" value. In this case the entire area under the curve consists of area to the left of the mean, which is equal to

Figure 4.5. Pull-down window for Excel functions.

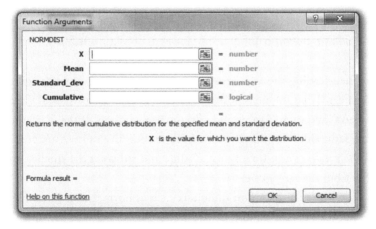

Figure 4.6. Excel window for normal distribution.

half the entire area or 0.5. That is why we are subtracting 0.5 to obtain the area from the mean to point 1.49.

Alternatively, point to the arrow on the side of the "Σ AutoSum" on Excel's command ribbon and choose "more function." From the drop-down menu choose "Statistical" in the window labeled "or select a category" and scroll down until you get to NORMDIST command.

Then scroll down until you see NORMDIST. Upon selecting the option, a new window opens up as shown in Figure 4.6.

Place the appropriate values in the correct boxes and press OK. If you look at the resulting cell, you will see the formula shown previously, except for 0.5, which we added to convert the result to a value between zero and a Z value. When using Excel, write the problem as in the forms shown previously, mark the area under the curve, and then decide if you are subtracting 0.5, adding probabilities, or subtracting them based on the shaded area.

Area Under a Normal Distribution with any Mean and Variance

Convert all normal distributions to the standard normal by standardizing all values.

1. Rewrite the question using probability notations.
2. Convert the values into Z scores. Do not forget the probability.
3. Draw a graph and shade the area under investigation.
4. Look up the probability or use Excel to obtain probability.

When finding the area between two Z values, if Z values are on two sides of zero, that is, one is positive and the other is negative, find the area between 0 and each Z value and **add** the probabilities. If the Z values are on the same side of 0, that is, either both are negative or both are positive, find the area between 0 and each Z value and **subtract** the smaller probability from the larger one.

Continuous distribution functions such as normal distribution share two concepts: (1) length and (2) area. The Z score is a measure of length. It shows how far a point is from the center (mean) of standard normal in terms of standard deviations. In other words, Z score indicates the number of units a point deviates from the mean. The probability of a particular Z value from the mean is an area. The area between mean (zero) and a point is the value provided in the standard normal table.

Example 4.1

Assume that the random variable X has a normal distribution with mean 16.9 and standard deviation of 3.01. Find

1. $P(X < 22.51)$
2. $P(X > 11.3)$
3. $P(13.93 < X < 23.41)$
4. $P(11.43 < X < 15.61)$
5. $P(17.64 < X < 21.45)$

Solution

The first step is to standardize the values, both alphabetically and numerically.

1. $P(X < 22.51) = P\left(\dfrac{X - \mu}{\sigma} > \dfrac{22.51 - 16.9}{3.01}\right) = P(Z < 1.86)$
$$= P(0 < Z < 1.86) + 0.5 = 0.4689 + 0.5 = 0.9689$$

Note that the area of interest is everything to the left of 1.86.

Alternatively, the Excel formula below will give the same answer:

$$=\text{NORMDIST}(22.51, 16.9, 3.01, 1) = 0.9689$$

2. $P(X > 11.3) = P\left(\dfrac{X - \mu}{\sigma} > \dfrac{11.3 - 16.9}{3.01}\right) = P(Z > -1.86)$
$$= P(-1.86 < Z < 0) + 0.5 = 0.4689 + 0.5 = 0.9689$$

Alternatively, the Excel formula below will give the same answer:

$$=\text{NORMDIST}(22.51, 16.9, 3.01, 1) = 0.9689$$

3. $P(13.93 < X < 23.41) = P\left(\dfrac{13.93 - 16.9}{3.01} < \dfrac{X - \mu}{\sigma} < \dfrac{23.41 - 16.9}{3.01}\right)$
$$= P(-0.99 < Z < 2.16)$$
$$= P(-0.99 < Z < 0) + P(0 < z < 2.16)$$
$$= 0.3389 + 0.4846 = 0.8235$$

(Continued)

(*Continued*)

4. $P(11.43 < X < 15.61) = P\left(\dfrac{11.43 - 16.9}{3.01} < \dfrac{X - \mu}{\sigma} < \dfrac{15.61 - 16.9}{3.01}\right)$

$= P(-1.82 < Z < -0.43)$

$= P(-1.82 < Z < 0) - P(0 < Z < -0.43)$

$= 0.4656 - 0.1664 = 0.2992$

5. $P(17.64 < X < 21.45) = P\left(\dfrac{17.64 - 16.9}{3.01} < \dfrac{X - \mu}{\sigma} < \dfrac{21.45 - 16.9}{3.01}\right)$

$= P(0.25 < Z < 1.51)$

$= P(0 < Z < 1.51) - P(0 < Z < 0.25)$

$= 0.4345 - 0.0987 = 0.5332$

Example 4.2

Let the random variable X have a normal distribution with mean 15 and standard deviation of 3.

1. What is the cut off value for the top 1% of this population?
2. Find the interquartile range.

Solution

1. In this example, the probability of the outcome is given and the value that determines the desired probability is the objective.

$$P(Z > z) = 0.01$$

where the lowercase z represents a specific value. Search for the probability that corresponds to $0.5 - 0.01 = 0.49$ in the body of the normal table. The Z score that corresponds to the probability of 0.49 is $Z = 2.325$.

Next, determine the X value by reversing the computation of the Z score.

(*Continued*)

(*Continued*)

$$Z = \frac{X - \mu}{\sigma} = \frac{X - 15}{3} = 2.325$$

$$X = 21.975$$

Therefore, 1% of the population has an X value greater than 21.975. Note that 21.975 is the 99th percentile.

2. For the first quartile:

$$P(Z < -z_1) = 0.25$$
$$P(-z_1 < Z < 0) = 0.5 - 0.25 = 0.25$$

Search the body of the table for 0.25. The closest number is 0.2502 that corresponds to the Z score of $z_1 = -0.675$. In the Z score formula solve for the value of X.

$$Z = \frac{X - \mu}{\sigma} = \frac{X - 15}{3} = -0.675$$

Therefore $X = 12.975$ is the first quartile.
    For the third quartile:

$$P(Z < z_3) = 0.75$$
$$P(0 < Z < z_3) = 0.75 - 0.5 = 0.25$$

From the above $z_3 = +0.675$

$$Z = \frac{X - \mu}{\sigma} = \frac{X - 15}{3} = +0.675$$

and hence the third quartile is:

$$X = 17.025$$

The middle 50% of the population lies between 12.975 and 17.025.

(*Continued*)

(*Continued*)

Solution Using Excel

1. Note that in Excel the top 1% is entered as 0.99 for probability.

    Point to the arrow on the side of the "Σ AutoSum" on Excel's ribbon command and choose the "more function." From the drop-down window choose "Statistical" in the window labeled "or select a category" and scroll down until you get to the NORMINV command (see Figure 4.5).

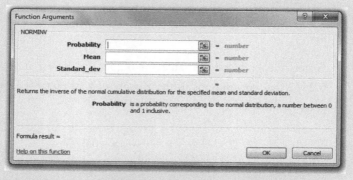

Figure 4.7. Excel window for inverse normal values.

Place the appropriate values in the correct boxes and press OK.

   The result 21.97904 is displayed, which is slightly different from the result from the table due to roundoff error. You could have entered the following formula as well.

   = NORMINV(0.99,15,3)

2.

   = NORMINV(0.25,15,3) = 12.97653
   = NORMINV(0.75,15,3) = 17.02347

   Again the results are slightly different due to roundoff error. Interestingly, both the above values and the values for the normal distribution table are obtained from Excel.

Nonconformity with Normal Distribution

Normality Versus Skewness

Normal distribution is the cornerstone of statistical analysis. The exact shape of the normal curve depends on the probability density function of the normal distribution. Any deviation from the normal probability density function results in skewness or Kurtosis. It is easy to detect skewness visually because skewed distributions are not symmetric. As a member of continuous symmetric distribution functions, the normal distribution function has the property that its mean, mode, and median coincide. The relationships between these three measures were provided in Chapter 3 for positively and negatively skewed distributions. In the subsequent graph, the positive and negatively skewed functions are superimposed on the normal distribution for comparison.

Normality Versus Kurtosis

Kurtosis measures the degree of flatness or pointedness of a symmetric curve as compared to a normal distribution. There is a formal measure

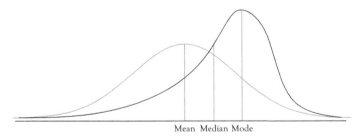

Mean Median Mode

Figure 4.8. Comparison of negative skewness with normal distribution.

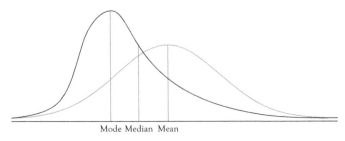

Mode Median Mean

Figure 4.9. Comparison of positive skewness with normal distribution.

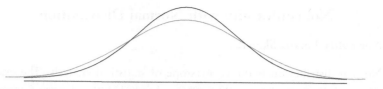

Figure 4.10. Comparison of negative Kurtosis (Platykurtic or flatter) with normal.

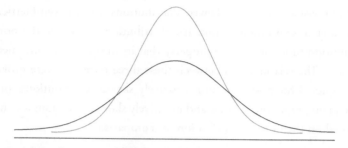

Figure 4.11. Comparison of positive Kurtosis (Leptokurtic or pointed) with normal.

of Kurtosis but involves the concept of the moment of a function which is beyond the scope of this text. However, it is beneficial to depict the graph of a flatter curve, called Platykurtic, which corresponds to a Kurtosis measure with negative value. A more peaked curve, called Leptokurtic corresponds to a Kurtosis measure with a positive value. Figures 4.10 and 4.11 represent comparisons to the normal curve.

Chi-Squared Distribution Function

Theorem 4.1

Let the random variable X have a normal distribution with mean and positive variance:

$$X \sim N(\mu, \sigma^2)$$

Then, the random variable

$$V = \frac{(X - \mu)^2}{\sigma^2}$$

will have a chi-squared (χ^2) distribution with one (1) degree of freedom.

$$V \sim \chi^2 (1)$$

Note that $Z = X - \mu/\sigma$ hence Z^2 is a $\chi^2 (1)$. Therefore, the normal values can be squared to obtain probabilities for the chi-square distribution with 1 degree of freedom.

$$P(|Z| < 1.96) = 0.956$$
$$P(Z^2 < (1.96)^2) = P(Z^2 = 3.842) = 0.95$$

This is identical to the chi-square value with one degree of freedom. Therefore, in confidence intervals and tests of hypotheses one can use either normal distribution or a chi-square distribution. Each one, however, would be beneficial in different settings.

Theorem 4.2

Let $X_1, X_2, \ldots, X_n$ be a random sample of size n from a distribution $N(\mu, \sigma^2)$. Recall

$$\hat{\mu} = \frac{\sum x}{n} \quad \text{and} \quad \widehat{\sigma^2} = \frac{\sum(x - \hat{\mu})^2}{n-1}$$

Therefore

  i. $\hat{\mu}$ and $\widehat{\sigma^2}$ are independent.

  ii. $\dfrac{(n-1)\widehat{\sigma^2}}{\sigma^2}$ is distributed as a **chi-squared with (n − 1) degrees of freedom.**

$$\frac{(n-1)\widehat{\sigma^2}}{\sigma^2} \sim \chi^2 (n-1)$$

The chi-square distribution is a special case of a gamma distribution. In a gamma distribution with parameters α and θ, let $\alpha = r/2$ and $\theta = 2$ where r is a positive integer. The resulting distribution function will be a chi-square distribution with r degrees of freedom. The mean will be r and the variance will be $2r$.

t Distribution Function

Theorem 4.3

Let X be a random variable that is $N(0, 1)$, and let U be a random variable that is $\chi^2(r)$. Assume Z and U are independent. Then

$$t = \frac{X}{\sqrt{\dfrac{U}{r}}}$$

(4.1)

has a **t distribution with r degrees of freedom.**

Theorem 4.4

Let X be a random variable that is $N(\mu, \sigma^2)$. Use the customary hat-notation to represent sample mean and sample variance. Then the following relationship has a **t distribution with (n − 1) degrees of freedom.**

$$t = \frac{\dfrac{(\hat{\mu} - \mu)}{\dfrac{\sigma}{\sqrt{n}}}}{\sqrt{\dfrac{(n-1)\widehat{\sigma^2}}{(n-1)\sigma^2}}} \sim t_{(n-1)}$$

(4.2)

When population variance is not known, using normal distribution for inference is misleading. The problem is more acute when the sample size is small.

F Distribution Function

Theorem 4.5

Let U and V be independent chi-square variables with r_1 and r_2 degrees of freedom, respectively. Then

$$F = \frac{U/r_1}{V/r_2}$$

(4.3)

has an **F distribution with r_1, r_2 degrees of freedom.**

$$\frac{U/r_1}{V/r_2} \sim F_{r_1, r_2}$$

The relation between F and Z is that

$$F = e^{2Z} \qquad\qquad (4.4)$$

The F Statistics consists of the ratio of two variables, each with a chi-squared, χ^2, distribution divided by their corresponding degrees of freedom.

CHAPTER 5

Sampling Distribution of Sample Statistics

Sampling

A sample is a subset of population that is collected in a variety of ways. The process of collecting samples is called sampling. As will become evident in this chapter, random sampling is very important for establishing the necessary theories for statistical analysis. For example, if a firm has 500 employees and 300 of them are men, then the probability of choosing a male worker at random is $300/500 = 0.60$ or 60%. Sampling techniques are not limited to random sampling. Each sampling technique has its advantages and disadvantages. This text is not going to focus on various sampling techniques. After a brief discussion about sampling, the focus will be on the properties and advantages of random sampling. Theories that are necessary for performing statistical inferences and are related to sampling are discussed in this chapter. In Chapter 2, we explained statistics and defined it as:

> *Statistics* is a numeric fact or summary obtained from a sample. It is always known, because it is calculated by the researcher, and it is a variable. Usually, statistics is used to make an inference about the corresponding population parameter.

The only way to know the parameters of a population is to conduct a census. Conducting a census is expensive and, contrary to common belief, is not always accurate. Since a census takes time, it is possible that the findings are already inaccurate by the time the massive information is obtained and verified for mistakes and tabulated. On average, it takes about 2 years or more to release the census results in the United States. During this time, all variables of collected data change; for example, new babies are born, some people die, and others move. Sampling, on the other hand, can be performed in a shorter amount of time, while occasionally the census information is sampled in order to release some of the results quicker.

Sometimes, taking a census is not an option. This is not only due to the time and money involved, but also because the census itself might be destructive. For example, in order to find out the average life of light bulbs, they must be turned on and left until they burn out. Barring mistakes, this would provide the average life of the light bulbs, but then there will not be any light bulbs left. Similarly, determining if oranges were not destroyed by frost requires cutting them up. Other examples abound. Conversely, there are lots of other reasons where it is unrealistic, if not impossible, to conduct a census to obtain information about a population and its parameters.

Collecting sample data is neither inexpensive nor effortless. Sampling textbooks devote many pages of explanation on how to obtain random samples from a population. One simple, but not necessarily pragmatic or efficient way, is to assign ID numbers to all members of the population. Then pull the desired number of sample points by drawing lots at random of the ID numbers.

In this instance, our interest in sampling is very limited. We are interested in obtaining an estimate from a relatively small portion of a population to obtain insight about its parameter. The knowledge of parameters allows meaningful analysis of the nature of the characteristics of interest in the population and is vital for making decisions about the population of the study.

As discussed earlier, summary values obtained from a sample are called **statistics**. Since statistics are variables, different samples result in slightly different outcomes and the values of statistics differ, which is the consequence of being a random variable. It is possible to have many samples and thus many sample statistics, for example, a **mean**. It turns out that the sample means have certain properties that are very useful. These properties allow us to conduct **statistical inference**.

Definition 5.1

Statistical inference is the method of using sample statistics to make conclusions about a population parameter.

Statistical inference requires the population of interest to be defined clearly and exclusively. Furthermore, the sample must be **random** in order to allow every member of the population an equal chance to appear in the sample, and to be able to take advantage of statistical theories and methods. Later, we will cover the theories that demonstrate why random sampling provides sufficient justification for making inferences about population parameters.

The method of using information from a sample to make inference about a population is called **inductive statistics**. In inductive statistics, we observe specifics to make an inference about the general population. This chapter introduces the necessary theories, while the remaining chapters provide specific methods for making inferences under different situations. We also use **deductive** methods in statistics. In deductive methods, we start from the general and make assertions about the specific.

Statistical inference makes probabilistic statements about the expected outcome. It is essential to realize that since random events occur probabilistically, there is no "certain" or "definite" statement about the outcome. Therefore, it is essential to provide the probability of the outcome associated with the expected outcome.

Sample Size

Before we discuss the role of randomness and the usefulness or effectiveness of a sample, it is important to understand how other factors influence the effectiveness of the sample statistics by providing **reliable** inference about a population parameter. Even if a sample is chosen at random, two other factors attribute to the reliability of the sample statistics. They are the variance of the population and the sample size. For a population with identical members, the necessary sample size is one. For example, if the output of a firm is always the same, say 500 units per day, then choosing any single given day at random would be sufficient to determine the firm's output. Note that in the previous example, there was no need to sample at random, although one can argue that any day that is chosen is a random day. However, if the output changes every day due to random factors such as sickness, mistakes during production, or breakdown of equipment, then sample size must increase. It is important to understand the possible difference in output among the days of the week and the month, if applicable. For example, Mondays and Fridays might have lower output. By Friday, workers might be tired and not as productive. Machinery might break or need to be cleaned more often towards the end of the week. On Mondays, workers might be sluggish and cannot perform up to their potential. Workers might be preoccupied towards the end of the month or early in the month when they are running out of money, or when their bills are due. These are just some of the issues that might have to be considered when setting up sampling techniques in order to assure the randomness of the sampled units. Therefore, there should be a direct relationship between the sample size and the variance of the population, and larger samples must be taken from populations with larger variance. Since statistical inference is probabilistic to obtain higher levels of confidence, we should take larger samples.

It can be shown that the required sample size for estimating a mean is given by:

$$n = \frac{Z_{a/2}^2 \, \sigma^2}{E^2} \tag{5.1}$$

where, $Z_{a/2}^2$ is the square of the Z score for desired level of significance,

σ^2 is the variance of the population,

E^2 is the square of tolerable level of error.

Example 5.1

Assume that the population's standard deviation for the output level is 29. Also, assume that we desire to limit our error to 5%, which makes the level of significance 95%. Let's allow the tolerable level of error to be 5.

To obtain the sample size, we first need to obtain the Z score. In Figure 5.1, the area in the middle is 95%. Therefore, the area at the two tails is equal to 0.05.

(Continued)

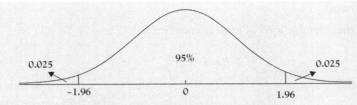

Figure 5.1. Graph of a normal distribution.

Furthermore, the area between zero and the right-hand cutoff point is 0.45, which according to the table corresponds with a Z score of 1.96. In Excel, you could use the following formula:

$$=\text{NORMINV} (0.975,0,1)$$

Note that the answer from Excel is 1.959964, which is slightly off. The necessary sample size is given by:

$$n = \frac{(1.96^2)(29^2)}{5^2} = \frac{3.84 \times 841}{25} = 129.23$$

Since fractional samples are not possible, we must always use the next integer to assure the desired level of accuracy. Therefore, the minimum sample size should be 130.

Definition 5.2

The **reliability** of a sample mean ($\hat{\mu}$) is equal to the probability that the deviation of the sample mean from the population mean is within the **tolerable level of error** (E):

$$\text{Reliability} = P (-E \leq \hat{\mu} - \mu \leq E) \qquad (5.2)$$

Example 5.2

A 95% reliability for the sample mean is given by the area between the two vertical lines in Figure 5.2.

$$\text{Reliability} = P (\mu - E (-E \leq \hat{\mu} - \mu \leq E) = 0.95$$

(*Continued*)

(*Continued*)

And the tolerable level of error is equal to:

$$E = 1.96 \frac{\sigma}{\sqrt{n}}$$

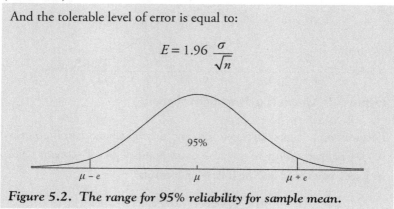

Figure 5.2. The range for 95% reliability for sample mean.

An astute student will notice that in order to estimate the sample size, it is necessary to know the variance. It is also imperative to understand that in order to calculate variance, one needs the mean, which apparently, is not available; otherwise we would not have to estimate it. Sometimes one might have enough evidence to believe that the variance for a population has not changed, while its mean has shifted. For example, everybody in a country is heavier, but the spread of the weights is no different than those in the past. In situations that the known variance is also believed to have changed, the only solution is to take a pre-sample to have a rough idea about the mean and variance of the population and then use sample estimates as a starting point to determine a more reliable sample size.

Sampling Distribution of Statistics

As stated earlier, sample statistics are a random variable and change from sample to sample. This means that the actual observed statistics is only one outcome of all the possible outcomes. A **sampling distribution** of any statistics explains how the statistics differ from one sample to another. The most commonly used statistics are sample mean and sample variance. Therefore, we will study their sampling distributions by approaching this subject in a systematic way. We begin with sampling distribution for one sample mean and distinguish between the cases when population variance is known and when it is unknown. Next, we introduce two sample means and address the cases of known and unknown variances, and so on. However, before embarking on this mission, it is necessary to discuss the Law of Large Numbers and the Central Limit Theorem, which are the foundations of inferential statistics.

Theorem 5.1 Law of Large Numbers

For a sequence of independent and identically distributed random variables, each with mean (μ) and variance (σ^2), the probability that the difference between the sample mean and population mean is greater than an arbitrary small number will approach zero as the number of samples approaches infinity.

The theorem indicates that as the number of random samples increase, the average of their means approaches the population's mean. Since sample means are statistics and random, their values change and none of them is necessarily equal to the population mean. The law of large numbers is essential for the Central Limit Theorem.

Theorem 5.2 Central Limit Theorem

Let θ be a population parameter. Let $\hat{\theta}$ be the estimated value of θ that is obtained from a sample. If we repeatedly sample at random from this population, the variable $\hat{\theta}$ will have the following properties:

1. The distribution function of $\hat{\theta}$ can be approximated by **normal distribution**
2. $E(\hat{\theta}) = \theta$
3. $\sigma_{\hat{\theta}}^2 = \dfrac{\sigma^2}{n}$

Property number 2, above, states that the expected value of the sample statistics ($\hat{\theta}$) will be equal to the population parameter (θ). In other words, the average of all such sample statistics will equal the actual value of the population parameter. Note that as the sample size increases, the sample variance of the estimate ($\sigma_{\hat{\theta}}^2$) decreases. Therefore, as the sample size increases, the sample statistics (estimate) gets closer and closer to the population parameter (θ).

The approximation improves when the sample size is large and the population **variance is known**. When the population **variance is unknown** and the sample size is small, then the sample statistics $\hat{\theta}$ will have the following properties:

1. The distribution function of $\hat{\theta}$ can be approximated by *t* **distribution** with $(n-1)$ degrees of freedom
2. $E(\hat{\theta}) = \theta$
3. $\widehat{\sigma_{\hat{\theta}}^2} = \dfrac{\sigma^2}{n}$

As the sample size increases, the distinction between normal distribution and *t* distribution vanishes.

The general population parameter θ can be the mean (μ), the proportion (π), or the variance (σ^2). For each of the above three parameters, we may be dealing with one or two populations (comparison). In each case, the mean and variance of the estimator will be different. There will be 10 different cases, which can be viewed in a summary table.

Lemma 5.1

Let $Y = X_1 + X_2 + \cdots + X_n$, where the Xs are random variables with a finite mean (μ) and a finite and **known** positive variance (σ^2). Then,

$$\frac{Y - \mu}{\sigma}$$

has a standard normal distribution, which indicates that it is a normal distribution with mean $= 0$ and variance $= 1$.

Sampling Distribution of One Sample Mean

Population Variance Is Known

Sample mean is a statistics. Assume we know the variance of a population from which the sample mean is obtained. Let $(\hat{\mu})$ be the mean of a random sample of size n from a distribution with a finite mean (μ) and a finite and **known** positive variance (σ^2). Using the central limit theorem, we know the following is true about the sample mean ($\hat{\mu}$):

1. The distribution function for ($\hat{\mu}$) can be approximated by the normal distribution (since the population variance is known)
2. $E(\hat{\mu}) = \mu$
3. $\sigma_{\hat{\mu}}^2 = \dfrac{\sigma^2}{n}$

Therefore, we can use the normal table values for comparison of the standardized values of the sample mean. The knowledge of population variance σ^2 is essential for completion of the third outcome. The distribution function of sample mean for samples of size 30 will be close to normal distribution. For random variables from a population that is symmetric, unimodal, and of the continuous type, a sample of size 4 or 5 might result in a very close approximation to normal distribution. If the population is approximately normal, then the sample mean would have a normal distribution when sample size is as little as 2 or 3.

Example 5.3

Assume that the variance for daily production of a good is 2800 pounds. Find the sampling distribution of the sample mean ($\hat{\mu}$) for a sample of size 67.

Solution
1. The sampling distribution of sample mean ($\hat{\mu}$) is normal
2. $E(\hat{\mu}) = \mu$
3. $\sigma_{\hat{\mu}}^2 = \dfrac{2800}{67} = 41.79$

As we see, there is very little computation involved. Nevertheless, the theoretical application is tremendous.

Example 5.4

Assume that the variance for daily production of a good is 2800 pounds. What is the probability that in a sample of 67 randomly selected days the output is 15 pounds, or more, below average?

Solution

We are interested in a deviation from the population average.

$$P[(\hat{\mu} = \mu) < -15] = P\left[\frac{(\hat{\mu} - \mu)}{\sqrt{\frac{\sigma^2}{n}}} < \frac{600 - 15}{\sqrt{\frac{2800}{67}}}\right]$$

$$= P\left[Z < \frac{-15}{\sqrt{41.79}}\right] = P\left[Z < \frac{-15}{6.47}\right]$$

$$= P[Z < 2.32] = 0.5 - P[Z > 2.32]$$

$$= 0.5 - 0.4898 = 0.0102$$

Note that for this problem, we do not need to know the true population mean since we are interested in knowing the probability of producing below the population mean.

Population Variance Is Unknown

Let $(\hat{\mu})$ be the mean of a random sample of size n from a distribution with a finite mean and a finite and **unknown** positive variance (σ^2). According to the Central Limit Theorem:

1. The distribution of $(\hat{\mu})$ can be approximated by a **t distribution** function
2. $E(\hat{\mu}) = \mu$
3. $\widehat{\sigma_{\hat{\mu}}^2} = \frac{\widehat{\sigma^2}}{n}$

Therefore, we can use the **t table** values, which are provided in the Appendix for comparison of the standardized values of the sample mean.

When the population size is small, or if the sample size to population size n/N is greater than 5%, you should use a **correction factor with the variance**. The correction factor is $N - n/N - 1$. For finite populations, the variance of the sample mean becomes:

$$\sigma_{\hat{\mu}}^2 = \frac{\sigma^2}{n} \frac{N - n}{N - 1} \qquad \text{known variance}$$

$$\widehat{\sigma_{\hat{\mu}}^2} = \frac{\widehat{\sigma^2}}{n} \frac{N - n}{N - 1} \qquad \text{unknown variance}$$

Summary

Distribution function for one sample mean

	Distribution	Mean	Variance
Population Variance is known	Normal	μ	$\dfrac{\sigma^2}{n}$
Population Variance is unknown	t	μ	$\dfrac{\widehat{\sigma^2}}{n}$

Sampling Distribution of One Sample Proportion

Let $(\hat{\pi})$ be a proportion from a random sample of size n from a distribution with a finite proportion (π) and a finite positive variance (σ^2). When both $n\pi \geq 5$ and $n(1 - \pi) \geq 5$, then the following theorem is correct based on the Central Limit Theorem:

1. The distribution of $(\hat{\pi})$ can be approximated by a **normal** distribution function
2. $E\,(\hat{\pi}) = \pi$
3. $\sigma_{\hat{\pi}}^2 = \dfrac{\hat{\pi}(1 - \hat{\pi})}{n}$

Note that in order to obtain the variance of the sample proportion, we must estimate the population proportion using the sample proportion. Thus, $\sigma_{\hat{\pi}}^2 = \widehat{\sigma_{\hat{\pi}}^2}$.

Therefore, we can use the normal table values for comparison of the standardized values of the sample mean. Note that the symbol pi (π) is used to represent the sample proportion and has nothing to do with $\pi = 3.141593...$

An added advantage of using sampling distribution of sample proportion is that you can use normal approximation to estimate probability of outcome for **binomial distribution function** without direct computation or the use of binomial distribution tables. When both $n\pi \geq 5$ and $n(1 - \pi) \geq 5$ it is reasonable to approximate a binomial distribution using a normal distribution.

Sampling Distribution of Two Sample Means

The extension from the distribution function of a single sample mean to two or more means is simple and follows naturally. However, it is necessary to introduce appropriate theories.

Theorem 5.3 The Expected Value of Sum of Random Variables

Let $Y = X_1 + X_2 + \cdots + X_n$, where the Xs are random variables. The expected value of Y is equal to the sum of the expected values of Xs.

$$E(Y) = E(X_1) + E(X_2) + \cdots + E(X_n)$$

Theorem 5.3 does not require that Xs be independent. This theorem allows us to sum two or more random variables.

Sampling Distribution of Difference of Two Means

When conducting inferences about two population parameters, there are two sample statistics, one from each population. Often, in order to conduct an inference the relationship between the parameters, and hence the corresponding statistics, has to be modified and written as either the difference of the parameters or the ratio of the parameters. This requires knowledge of the distribution function for the difference of two sample statistics or the distribution function for the ratio of two sample statistics.

In this section, the sampling distribution of the difference of two sample means is discussed. Choose a distribution function for the difference of two sample proportion or the distribution function for the ratio of two variances to access those distribution functions. This section will address the distribution function of the difference of two means.

The Two Sample Variances Are Known and Unequal

Let $(\widehat{\mu_1})$ and $(\widehat{\mu_2})$ be the means of two random samples of sizes n_1 and n_2 from distributions with finite means μ_1 and μ_2 and finite positive **known and unequal** variances σ_1^2 and σ_2^2. Let n_1 and n_2 be the respective sample sizes. According to the Central Limit Theorem and Theorem 5.3:

1. The distribution of $(\widehat{\mu_1} - \widehat{\mu_2})$ is normal
2. $E(\widehat{\mu_1} - \widehat{\mu_2}) = \mu_1 - \mu_2$
3. $Var(\widehat{\mu_1} - \widehat{\mu_2}) = \dfrac{\sigma_1^2}{n_1} + \dfrac{\sigma_2^2}{n_1}$.

Note that the variances of the two samples are added together, while the means are subtracted. Therefore, we can use the normal table values for comparison of the standardized values of the differences of sample means.

The Two Sample Variances Are Known and Equal

Let $(\widehat{\mu_1})$ and $(\widehat{\mu_2})$ be the means of two random samples of sizes n_1 and n_2 from distributions with finite means μ_1 and μ_2 and finite positive **known and equal** variances σ_1^2 and σ_2^2. Let n_1 and n_2 be the respective sample sizes. According to the Central Limit Theorem and Theorem 5.3:

1. The distribution of $(\widehat{\mu_1} - \widehat{\mu_2})$ is normal
2. $E(\widehat{\mu_1} - \widehat{\mu_2}) = \mu_1 - \mu_2$
3. $Var(\widehat{\mu_1} - \widehat{\mu_2}) = \sigma^2 \left(\dfrac{1}{n_1} + \dfrac{1}{n_2} \right)$

Since $\sigma_1^2 = \sigma_2^2 = \sigma^2$.

The Two Sample Variances Are Unknown and *Unequal*

Let $(\widehat{\mu_1})$ and $(\widehat{\mu_2})$ be the means of two random samples of sizes n_1 and n_2 from distributions with finite means μ_1 and μ_2 and finite positive **unknown and *unequal*** variances σ_1^2 and σ_2^2. Let n_1 and n_2 be the respective sample sizes. According to the Central Limit Theorem and Theorem 5.3:

1. The distribution of $(\widehat{\mu_1} - \widehat{\mu_2})$ is normal
2. $E\ (\widehat{\mu_1} - \widehat{\mu_2}) = \mu_1 - \mu_2$

3. $Var\ (\widehat{\mu_1} - \widehat{\mu_2}) = \dfrac{\widehat{\sigma_1^2}}{n_1} + \dfrac{\widehat{\sigma_2^2}}{n_2}$

The Two Sample Variances Are Unknown and *Equal*

Let $(\widehat{\mu_1})$ and $(\widehat{\mu_2})$ be the means of two random samples of sizes n_1 and n_2 from distributions with finite means μ_1 and μ_2 and finite positive **unknown and *equal*** variances σ_1^2 and σ_2^2. Let n_1 and n_2 be the respective sample sizes. According to the Central Limit Theorem and Theorem 5.3:

1. The distribution of $(\widehat{\mu_1} - \widehat{\mu_2})$ is normal
2. $E\ (\widehat{\mu_1} - \widehat{\mu_2}) = \mu_1 - \mu_2$

3. $Var\ \widehat{\mu_1} - \widehat{\mu_2} = \widehat{\sigma_{Pooled}^2} = \left(\dfrac{1}{n_1} + \dfrac{1}{n_2}\right)$

where $\sigma_{Pooled}^2 = \dfrac{(n_1 - 1)\widehat{\sigma_2^2} + (n_2 - 1)\widehat{\sigma_1^2}}{n_1 + n_2 - 2}$.

Summary of Sampling Distribution of Sample Means

Do not let these seemingly different and possibly difficult formulae confuse you. They are similar. The most common case is case 3, which is listed earlier. The first three cases can use this formula without any problem. The last case, earlier, takes advantage of the fact that there are two estimates of the unknown variance instead of one. Logic dictates that it would be better to average the two estimates using their respective sample sizes as weights. Table 5.1 provides a summary of

Table 5.1 Summary of Sampling Distribution for Sample Mean

Sample statistics	Population variance(s)	Distribution	Mean	Variance of sample statistics
$\hat{\mu}$	Known	Normal	μ	$\dfrac{\sigma^2}{n}$
$\hat{\mu}$	Unknown	t	μ	$\dfrac{\widehat{\sigma}^2}{n}$
$\widehat{\mu_1} - \widehat{\mu_2}$	Known and Unequal	Normal	$\mu_1 - \mu_2$	$\dfrac{\sigma_1^2}{n_1} + \dfrac{\sigma_2^2}{n_1}$
$\widehat{\mu_1} - \widehat{\mu_2}$	Known and Equal	Normal	$\mu_1 - \mu_2$	$\sigma^2\left(\dfrac{1}{n_1} + \dfrac{1}{n_2}\right)$
$\widehat{\mu_1} - \widehat{\mu_2}$	Unknown and Unequal	t	$\mu_1 - \mu_2$	$\dfrac{\widehat{\sigma_1^2}}{n_1} + \dfrac{\widehat{\sigma_2^2}}{n_2}$
$\widehat{\mu_1} - \widehat{\mu_2}$	Unknown an Equal	t	$\mu_1 - \mu_2$	$\widehat{\sigma_{Pooled}^2}\left(\dfrac{1}{n_1} + \dfrac{1}{n_2}\right)$

sample statistics, its distribution functions, and its parameters for one and two sample means.

Sampling Distribution of Difference of Two Proportions

When conducting inferences about two population parameters there are two sample statistics, one from each population. Often, in order to conduct an inference, the relationship between the parameters, and hence the corresponding statistics, has to be modified and written as either the difference of the parameters or the ratio of the parameters. This requires knowledge of the distribution function for the difference of two sample statistics or the distribution function of the ratio of two sample statistics. In this section, sampling distribution of the difference of two sample proportions is discussed. Choose the distribution function for the difference of two means or the distribution function for the ratio of two variances to access distribution functions for differences of two means or the ratio of two variances. This section will address the distribution function of the difference of two proportions.

Let $\widehat{\pi_1}$ and $\widehat{\pi_2}$ be the proportions of interest in two random samples of sizes n_1 and n_2 from distributions with finite proportions π_1 and π_2

Table 5.2. Summary of Sampling Distributions of Sample Proportions

Sample statistics	Population variance(s)	Distribution	Mean	Variance of sample statistics
$\hat{\pi}$	NA	Normal	π	$\dfrac{\hat{\pi}(1-\hat{\pi})}{n_1}$
$\hat{\pi_1}-\hat{\pi_2}$	NA	Normal	$\pi_1-\pi_2$	$\dfrac{\hat{\pi_1}(1-\hat{\pi_1})}{n_1}+\dfrac{\hat{\pi_2}(1-\hat{\pi_2})}{n_2}$

and finite positive variances σ_1^2 and σ_2^2. According to the Central Limit Theorem:

1. The distribution of $(\hat{\pi_1}-\hat{\pi_2})$ is normal
2. $E(\hat{\pi_1}-\hat{\pi_2})=\pi_1-\pi_2$
3. $Var(\hat{\pi_1}-\hat{\pi_2})=\dfrac{\hat{\pi_1}(1-\hat{\pi_1})}{n_1}+\dfrac{\hat{\pi_2}(1-\hat{\pi_2})}{n_2}$

Therefore, we can use the normal table values for comparison of the standardized values of the sample mean.

In practice, $\pi_1-\pi_2$ is not known and their estimates, $\hat{\pi_1}$ and $\hat{\pi_2}$ respectively, are used in calculating the variance of $(\hat{\pi_1}-\hat{\pi_2})$. The distribution function, expected value, and standard deviation for one and two sample proportions are given in Table 5.2.

Sampling Distribution of Sample Variance

Theorem 5.4

Let the random variable X have normal distribution with mean μ and variance σ^2, then random variable

$$V=\left(\frac{X-\mu}{\sigma}\right)^2=Z^2$$

has a chi-squared distribution with one (1) degree of freedom, which is shown as $\chi^2(1)$. Z is the same Z score as discussed in previous chapters, which consists of individual error divided by average error.

Chi-squared distributions are cumulative. Therefore, when n chi-squared distribution functions are added up, the result is another chi-squared distribution with n (sum of n distribution functions each with one) degree of freedom.

Theorem 5.5

Let random variables X_1, X_2, ..., X_n have normal distribution each with mean μ and variance σ^2 then the sum $\Sigma\left(\dfrac{X-\mu}{\sigma}\right)^2$ has a chi-squared distribution with n degrees of freedom. From this relation, we can build confidence intervals for one and two variances, and test hypothesis for one and two variances.

Sampling Distribution of Two Samples Variances

When conducting inferences about two population parameters, there are two sample statistics, one from each population. Often, in order to conduct an inference, the relationship between the parameters, and hence the corresponding statistics, has to be modified and written as either the difference of the parameters or the ratio of the parameters. This requires knowledge of the distribution function of the difference of two sample statistics or the distribution function of the ratio of two sample statistics. In this section, the sampling distribution of the ratio of two sample variances is discussed. Choose the distribution function for difference of two means or the distribution function for difference of two proportions to access distribution functions for differences of means or proportions. This section will address the distribution function of the ratio of two variances.

Theorem 5.6

Let random variables X_1, X_2, ..., X_m have normal distribution each with mean μ_1 and variance σ_1^2 and the random variable Y_1, Y_2, ..., Y_n have normal distribution each with mean μ_2 and variance σ_2^2 then random variable

$$F = \Sigma\left(\frac{X - \mu_1}{\sigma}\right)^2 \bigg/ \Sigma\left(\frac{Y - \mu_2}{\sigma}\right)^2$$

has an F distribution with m and n degrees of freedom.

Note that in Theorem 5.6, we could have expressed the numerator and denominator in terms of the corresponding chi-square distributions as stated in Theorem 5.5, which in turn is built upon Theorem 5.4.

In practice, when populations are not known, they are substituted by their respective sample variances.

$$F = \frac{\sigma_1^2}{\sigma_2^2}$$

It is assumed that the variance labeled σ_1^2 is greater than the variance labeled σ_2^2. Tabulated values of F are greater than or equal to 1.

The most common use of F distribution at this level is for the test of hypothesis of equality of two variances. This test provides a way of determining whether or not to pool variances when testing for the equality of two means with unknown population variances. First, test the equality of variances. If the hypothesis is rejected, then the variances are different and are not pooled. If the hypothesis is not rejected, then the variances are the same and must be pooled to obtain a weighted average of the two estimated values

Another use of F distribution is in testing three or more means. When testing a hypothesis that involves more than two means, we cannot use the t distribution. Test of hypothesis and the use of t and F distributions are discussed in Chapter 6.

Efficiency Comparison Between Mean and Median

Let $\hat{\mu}$ be the sample mean and $\hat{M}$ be the sample median. The **expected value** of, both, **sample mean** and **sample median** is equal to **population mean**. That is, both provide unbiased estimates of the population mean. However, as shown below, the sample mean is more efficient than the sample median in estimating the population mean. An estimator of a parameter is said to be more efficient than another estimator if the former has smaller variance. According to **Central Limit Theorem**, the variance of the sample mean ($\hat{\mu}$) is

$$\widehat{\sigma^2} = \frac{\sigma^2}{n}$$

It can be shown that the variance of the median is

$$\text{Variance (Sample Median)} = \frac{\pi\sigma^2}{2n}$$

where $\pi = 3.141593\ldots$

$$\frac{\text{Variance (Sample Mean)}}{\text{Variance (Sample Median)}} = \frac{\dfrac{\sigma^2}{n}}{\dfrac{\pi\sigma^2}{2n}} = \frac{2}{\pi} = \frac{2}{3.14159} = 0.64$$

Therefore, $\hat{\mu}$ is more efficient than median in estimating the population mean. The variance of the sample median from a sample of size 100 is about the same as the variance of the sample mean from a sample of size 64.

It is worthwhile to note the following discrepancy, which is caused by having a different orientation or starting point.

$$\text{Var }(\hat{M}) = 1.57 \text{ Var }(\hat{\mu})$$
$$\text{Var }(\hat{\mu}) = 0.6366 \text{ Var }(\hat{M})$$

Therefore, the variance of sample mean is only 64% of the variance of the sample median. In estimating population mean, if we take a sample of size 100 and use the sample mean as the estimator, we will get a certain variance and hence, an error. To obtain the same level of error using the sample median to estimate the population mean, we need a sample of 157, which is 1.57 times more than 100.

Recall that when extreme observations exist, sample median is preferred to sample mean because it is not influenced by extreme values.

For example, in real estate it is of interest to know the price of a typical house. The industry reports the prices of homes listed, sold, or withdrawn from the market each month. Usually, only a small fraction of existing homes is listed, sold, or withdrawn from the market. This causes large fluctuations in the average prices of these groups. The industry reports the median instead of the average price for the listings. Both sample mean and sample median are unbiased estimates of population mean, however, the latter is not influenced by the extreme high or low prices and thus is a better short-run estimator. Since sample median is less efficient than sample mean in estimating the population mean, larger samples are needed.

CHAPTER 6

Point and Interval Estimation

Estimation Versus Inference

There are two distinct ways of using statistics: Descriptive statistics and inferential statistics. Descriptive statistics provide summary statistics in the forms of tables, graphs, or computed values. We can use descriptive statistics to describe population data or sample data. Inferential statistics is used to draw conclusions about population parameters using sample statistics. Obtaining sample statistics for inferential statistics is the same as obtaining them for descriptive statistics. The use of the sample statistics determines whether it is descriptive or inferential. The statistics obtained from a sample for the purpose of inference is called **estimation**, to emphasize the fact that they are estimates for their respective parameters. In the previous chapters, the portions of descriptive statistics that dealt with samples are actually **estimations**. When we obtain sample mean, proportion, or variance we are calculating estimates of the corresponding population parameters. As we have demonstrated earlier, estimation is important. When sample estimates are used to test population parameters and to indicate how far the estimates are from parameters, then we are in the domain of inferential statistics. Some statisticians believe that the primary objective of statistics is to make **inferences** about population parameters using sample **statistics**. Using sample statistics to make deductions about population parameters is called **statistical inference**. Statistical inference can be based on **point estimation** or **confidence interval**, both of which will be covered shortly. They are closely related, and in some cases, they are interchangeable.

Point Estimation

A point estimate is the statistic obtained from a sample. The reason for the name is because the estimate consists of a single value. Examples of point estimates include sample **mean** ($\hat{\mu}$), sample **proportion** ($\hat{\pi}$), sample **variance** ($\widehat{\sigma^2}$), and sample median. These statistics are used to estimate the population mean (μ), population proportion (π), and population variance (σ^2), respectively. Sample **median** can be used to estimate, both, population median and population mean. In fact, any single-valued estimate obtained from a sample is a point estimate. Good estimates are close to the corresponding population parameter. Proper sampling provides accurate estimates of the unknown population parameter. Descriptive statistics addresses the procedure to obtain and calculate point estimates from the sample. It also explains their properties and uses. As discussed in Chapter 3, a suitable estimate is **unbiased**, **consistent**, and **efficient**.

Although point estimates are useful in providing descriptive information about a population, their usefulness is limited because we cannot determine how far they are from the targeted parameter. In order to provide levels of confidence and a probability for **margin of error** one needs to know the distribution function of sample statistics. Once a sampling distribution of the sample statistic is known, the probability of observing a certain sample statistic can be calculated with the aid of the corresponding table.

Example 6.1

Calculate point estimates of mean, median, variance, standard deviation, and coefficient of variation for the stock prices of Wal-Mart and Microsoft from March 12 to March 30, 2012.

Solution

The solutions are found by using Microsoft Excel. Refer to the Appendix on Excel.

(*Continued*)

Date	WMT	MSFT
12 Mar.	$60.68	$32.04
13 Mar.	$61.00	$32.67
14 Mar.	$61.08	$32.77
15 Mar.	$61.23	$32.85
16 Mar.	$60.84	$32.60
19 Mar.	$60.74	$32.20
20 Mar.	$60.60	$31.99
21 Mar.	$60.56	$31.91
22 Mar.	$60.65	$32.00
23 Mar.	$60.75	$32.01
26 Mar.	$61.20	$32.59
27 Mar.	$61.09	$32.52
28 Mar.	$61.19	$32.19
29 Mar.	$60.82	$32.12
30 Mar.	$61.20	$32.26
Mean	$60.89	$32.32
Variance	0.056464	0.10941
Median	$60.83	$32.20
St. Dev	0.237622	0.33078
CV	$0.0039	$0.0102

Interval Estimation

Statistics deals with random phenomena. Nothing remains constant in life. Methods of production change. Processes are modified. Machines get out of calibration. New techniques are applied. In all these cases, statistics is used to determine what remains constant and what changes. In estimation theory, sample statistics is used to estimate the population parameter. However, when one uses point estimation, it is not clear how close the estimate is to the parameter and there is no measure of confidence. This does not mean that point estimates are useless or unreliable. With proper sampling the point estimates will be unbiased, consistent, and efficient.

Interval estimation augments point estimates by providing a margin of error for the point estimate. The margin of error is a range, based on the degree of certainty, for the estimate of the population parameter, which is added and subtracted from a point estimate. Confidence intervals are based on the point estimate of the parameter and the distribution function of the point estimate. It is affected by the level of certainty, the variance of data, and the sample size.

Calculating Confidence Intervals

Interval estimation is a simple notion and is defined as:

$$\text{Point estimate} \pm \text{Margin of error} \tag{6.1}$$

In order to explain this concept we need to recall things from Chapters 2, 3, and 4. We covered point estimates in Chapter 2, although we did not use the same terminology. Point estimates are sample statistics and are used to estimate the corresponding population parameters. Mean, median, variance, and proportion are some common examples of point estimates.

The margin of error is not totally new either. It is based on the use of Z score, which we covered in Chapter 3. In Chapter 4 we introduced the normal distribution function and demonstrated the use of Z score and standardization in obtaining probabilities of random variables from normal distribution. Also in Chapter 4, we used a Z score to obtain the probability under normal distribution between two points. Previously we pointed out that due to symmetry of the standardized normal distribution, the probability of the area from zero, that is, the center, to a point on the right is equal to the probability of the area from zero to the negative value of that number (see Figure 6.1).

Note that in Figure 6.1, the mean is 0 and the standard deviation is 1. Also recall that the unit of measurement of the Z score is the standard deviation. Conventionally, we do not write 1 but if the standard deviation was different from 1, we must include that in the measure, as in Figure 6.1. Therefore, a point on the normal distribution curve is $Z\sigma$ away from the mean.

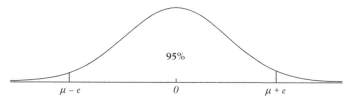

Figure 6.1. Margin of error on normal distribution.

When dealing with sample statistics, the properties of sampling distribution apply. Therefore, in the case of statistics, that is, estimates obtained from the sample, the Central Limit Theorem states that the standard deviation is given by $\sigma/\sqrt{n}$. Replacing σ with the this formula provides

$$\text{Margin of Error} = Z_{a/2} \frac{\sigma}{\sqrt{n}} \qquad (6.2)$$

It is very important to realize that the margin of error formula in Equation 6.2 depends on the knowledge of population variance. When the population variance is unknown and the sample variance has to be used, then the formula must be adjusted by replacing the population standard deviation with the sample standard deviation and the Z value must be replaced by the t value as in Equation 6.3:

$$\text{Margin of Error} = t_{a/2} \frac{\hat{\sigma}}{\sqrt{n}} \qquad (6.3)$$

Example 6.2

Calculate the margin of error for Microsoft stock price for the period March 12–March 30, 2012, using 83% level of confidence. Assume the real population variance is equal to the sample variance.

Solution

First obtain the Z value that corresponds to half of the 0.83 level of confidence so we can use the normal table provided in the Appendix to this book.

$$P(0 < Z < X) = \left(\frac{0.83}{2}\right) = 0.415$$

(Continued)

(*Continued*)

> Searching in the body of the normal table, we find the probability 0.415 corresponds roughly to $Z = 1.375$. Note that we are using the sample variance as if it was the **actual** population variance.
>
> According to Example 2.16 the variance of the data is 0.102.
>
> $$\text{Margin of Error} = 1.375\sqrt{\frac{0.102}{15}} = 1.375 \times 0.08239 = 0.1133$$
>
> However, since the population variance is unknown we must use the t value instead of Z value. Unfortunately, t values for alpha of $(1 - 0.83)/2 = 0.085$ are not readily available. However, Microsoft Excel provides the necessary number by using the following command:
>
> $$= t.\text{inv}(0.085, 14) = 1.44669$$
>
> Note that Excel will provide a negative sign in front of the t value because it refers to the left hand tail. But we do not need to worry, since the distribution is symmetric.
>
> Therefore, Margin of Error $= 1.44669 \times 0.2316 = 0.33505$
>
> This is the correct value of margin of error because it is using the t value, as required when population variance is unknown.

The concept of margin of error applies to sample statistics but not to the population parameters. Population parameters are constant values and do not have margin of error. However, sample statistics, which are random variables and are estimating their respective population parameters, have a margin of error. As seen in Equation 6.2, margin of error is **directly** related to variance of the population and the level of confidence, as indicated by the Z score, and **inversely** related to the square root of the sample mean.

Recall from Chapter 5 that the sampling distribution of sample mean is affected by the knowledge of the population variance. If the population variance is known, the distribution function of the sample mean is a **normal distribution**. However, if the population variance is not known the distribution function of the sample mean is a *t* **distribution**.

Therefore, when calculating the margin of error we must use either the normal table or the t table, depending on whether the population variance is known or unknown, respectively.

In Chapter 5, we learned the sampling distribution function of one sample statistics such as mean, proportion, and variance. When calculating margin of error for these statistics we need to use the appropriate distribution function. We learned the sampling distribution of the differences of two sample means and two sample proportions, both of which are a normal distribution. We also learned the sampling distribution of two variances, which is an F distribution. Once the margin of error is calculated, obtaining confidence interval is simple by using Equation 6.1.

Terminology

The probability between $-Z$ and $+Z$ from a standard normal, that is, a normal distribution with mean zero 0 and variance 1, is shown by $(1 - a)\%$. This is because the area outside of the above range is equal to a. In Chapter 7, we will provide more explanation for the naming of these areas and go into more detail on the meaning of the term a.

Customarily, normal distribution tables are calculated for half of the area, because of symmetry. Thus, the Z value, which corresponds to one half of a is shown as $Z_{a/2}$.

Interval Estimation for One Population Mean

The correct way of writing interval estimation of Equation 6.1 when estimating the population mean is

$$\hat{\mu} \pm Z_{a/2} \frac{\sigma}{\sqrt{n}} \qquad (6.4)$$

Definition 6.1

Based on Chapter 5, the $(1 - a)\%$ confidence interval for the **mean of one population** (μ) when the population **variance is known** is given by Equation (6.4).

Note that we need to calculate the following two values to obtain a confidence interval.

$$\text{Lower Bond: } \hat{\mu} - Z_{a/2} \frac{\sigma}{\sqrt{n}} \tag{6.5}$$

$$\text{Upper Bond: } \hat{\mu} + Z_{a/2} \frac{\sigma}{\sqrt{n}} \tag{6.6}$$

Sometimes we refer to the lower bond and upper bond as LB and UB, respectively.

Rule 6.1 Inference with Confidence Interval

The confidence interval covers the true population parameter with $(1-a)\%$ confidence.

Example 6.3

Provide an 83% confidence interval for Microsoft stock price for the period of March 12 to March 30, 2012. **Assume** the real population variance is equal to the sample variance.

Solution

From Examples 6.1 and 6.2 we have the necessary numbers.

LB = 32.32 – 0.1133 = 31.21
UB = 32.32 + 0.1133 = 32.43

An 83% confidence interval for the mean of Microsoft stock price between March 12 to March 30, 2012, is given by the range $31.21 to $32.43.

Note that we assumed the sample variance is equal to the population variance in order to apply the example to this case. If the variance is unknown, which is true more often than it is not, we have to use Equation 6.7. Furthermore, when the value of population variance is not known, we must use a t distribution value rather than a Z distribution value.

Definition 6.2

Based on Chapter 5, the $(1 - a)$% confidence interval for the **mean of one population** (μ) when the population **variance is unknown,** is given by the following equation:

$$\hat{\mu} \pm t_{a/2} \frac{\hat{\sigma}}{\sqrt{n}} \qquad (6.7)$$

In earlier days when t tables were only available for 1%, 5%, and 10% levels of significance, most researchers would use a normal table instead of the t table when sample size was greater than 30. With wide availability of t values for any level of significance, this practice is no longer necessary.

Example 6.4

Provide a 95% confidence interval for Microsoft stock price for the period of March 12 to March 30, 2012.

Solution

Since the population **variance is unknown** and the sample size is **less than 30,** we need to use the *t* **distribution.** The t value for 95% confidence interval is ±2.14479. To obtain this value look under 2.5% probability of type I error with 14 degrees of freedom in the t table or use the following Excel command.

$$= \text{t.inv}(.025,14) = -2.14479$$

The value reported by Excel is negative because it is designed to report the lower-end critical value.

Example 6.2 reported the appropriate standard deviation based on the variance calculated in Example 1.16.

$$\text{LB} = 32.32 - 2.14479 \, (0.8239) = 30.55291$$
$$\text{UB} = 32.32 + 2.14479 \, (0.8239) = 34.08709$$

A 95% confidence interval for the mean of Microsoft stock price is given by the range $30.55 to $34.09. This is the correct confidence interval because it uses the t value since the population variance is unknown.

Since *t* values are somewhat larger, to account for the fact that the population variance is unknown and must be estimated, the corresponding confidence interval is wider than the one calculated using a *Z* table when we assume to know the population variance.

Definition 6.3

Based on Chapter 5, the $(1 - a)\%$ confidence interval for the **proportion of one population** (π) is given by the following equation:

$$\hat{\pi} \pm Z_{a/2}\sqrt{\frac{\hat{\pi}(1 - \hat{\pi})}{n}} \tag{6.8}$$

Example 6.5

Calculate a 95% confidence interval for the proportion of stock prices of Microsoft that are higher than $32.5. Use the sample data from April 2 to April 21, 2012, provided in Example 3.2.

Solution

The sample proportion of stocks over $32.5 is

$$\hat{\pi} = \frac{4}{15} = 0.4$$

The *Z* value corresponding to 95% confidence is 1.96.

$$LB = 0.4 - 1.96\left(\sqrt{\frac{0.4 \times 0.6}{15}}\right) = 0.4 - 1.96 \times 0.1265 = 0.4 - 0.2479$$

$$= 0.1521$$

$$UB = 0.4 + 1.96\left(\sqrt{\frac{0.4 \times 0.6}{15}}\right) = 0.4 + 1.96 \times 0.1265 = 0.4 + 0.2479$$

$$= 0.6479$$

The range 0.1521 to 0.6479 covers the true population proportion of Microsoft stock prices that are $32.5 or higher.

(Continued)

Since the population variance is not known and the **sample size is smaller than 30**, we should have used the t distribution instead of normal distribution. In practice, the sample size is much larger when proportions are used. The results using the t values are given by:

$$LB = 0.4 - 2.145\left(\sqrt{\frac{0.4 \times 0.6}{15}}\right) = 0.4 - 2.145 \times 0.1265$$
$$= 0.4 - 0.2713 = 0.1287$$

$$UB = 0.4 + 2.145\left(\sqrt{\frac{0.4 \times 0.6}{15}}\right) 0.4 + 2.145 \times 0.1265$$
$$= 0.4 + 0.2713 = 0.6713$$

The range 0.1287 to 0.6713 covers the true population proportion of Microsoft stock prices that are $32.5 or higher. Note that the range became wider when we used the t distribution value. This is the consequence of not knowing the population variance.

Definition 6.4

Based on Chapter 5, the $(1 - a)\%$ confidence interval for the **difference** of **means of two populations** $(\mu_1 - \mu_2)$ when the population **variances are known and** *unequal* is given by the following equation:

$$\widehat{\mu_1} - \widehat{\mu_2} \pm Z_{a/2}\sqrt{\frac{\sigma_1^2}{n_1} + \frac{\sigma_2^2}{n_1}} \tag{6.9}$$

Definition 6.5

Based on Chapter 5, the $(1 - a)\%$ confidence interval for the **difference** of **means of two populations** $(\mu_1 - \mu_2)$ when the population **variances are known and** *equal* is given by the following equation:

$$(\widehat{\mu_1} - \widehat{\mu_2}) \pm Z_{a/2}\sqrt{\sigma^2\left(\frac{1}{n_1} + \frac{1}{n_2}\right)} \tag{6.10}$$

Definition 6.6

Based on Chapter 5, the $(1-a)\%$ confidence interval for the **difference** of **means of two populations** $(\mu_1-\mu_2)$ when the population **variances are unknown and *unequal*** is given by the following equation:

$$(\widehat{\mu_1} - \widehat{\mu_2}) \pm t_{a/2}\sqrt{\frac{\widehat{\sigma_1^2}}{n_1} + \frac{\widehat{\sigma_2^2}}{n_2}} \qquad (6.11)$$

Example 6.6

Obtain a 95% confidence interval for the difference in Microsoft stock prices between March 12 and March 30, 2012, and April 2 and April 21, 2012. The data is provided in Example 3.2.

Solution
Let's mark the data in March with the subscript "1" and those for April with subscript "2." The required formula is given in Equation 6.11. According to the formula we need the means and variances from both periods as well as the t value corresponding to 95% confidence.

We have the following results from previous examples. Make sure to verify the accuracy of the output. Remember that rounding off the numbers in early stages of calculation may produce discrepancies in final results. Here, we are using the output from Excel, which is somewhat larger than the values obtained using the computational method of Equation 2.35. The short-cut Equation 2.35 produces the least amount of rounding off, and thus is more accurate.

$$\widehat{\mu_1} = 32.32 \qquad \widehat{\sigma_1^2} = 0.10941$$

$$\widehat{\mu_2} = 31.27 \qquad \widehat{\sigma_2^2} = 0.372182$$

$$= t.inv(0.025,28) = -2.0484$$

(Continued)

Since we lose two degrees of freedom the correct degrees of freedom for the t distribution is $15 + 15 - 2 = 28$. Recall that we need to use both positive and negative t values.

$$LB = (\widehat{\mu_1} - \widehat{\mu_2}) - t_{a/2}\sqrt{\frac{\widehat{\sigma_1^2}}{n_1} + \frac{\widehat{\sigma_2^2}}{n_2}}$$

$$= (32.32 - 31.27) - 2.0484\sqrt{\frac{0.10941}{15} + \frac{0.372182}{15}}$$

$$= 1.05 - 2.0484\sqrt{0.007294 + 0.024812}$$

$$= 1.05 - 2.0484 \times 0.179183$$

$$= 1.05 - 0.36704 = \$0.68$$

$$UB = (\widehat{\mu_1} - \widehat{\mu_2}) - t_{a/2}\sqrt{\frac{\widehat{\sigma_1^2}}{n_1} + \frac{\widehat{\sigma_2^2}}{n_2}}$$

$$= (32.32 - 31.27) + 2.0484\sqrt{\frac{0.10941}{15} + \frac{0.372182}{15}}$$

$$= 1.05 + 2.0484\sqrt{0.007294 + 0.024812}$$

$$= 1.05 + 2.0484 \times 0.179183$$

$$= 1.05 + 0.36704 = \$1.42$$

The range \$0.68 to \$1.42 covers the difference of the means of the two periods of stock prices for Microsoft with 95% probability.

Definition 6.7

Based on Chapter 5, the $(1 - a)\%$ confidence interval for the **difference of means of two populations** $(\mu_1 - \mu_2)$ when the population **variances are unknown and *equal*** is given by the following equation:

$$(\widehat{\mu_1} - \widehat{\mu_2}) \pm t_{a/2}\sqrt{\widehat{\sigma_{Pooled}^2}\left(\frac{1}{n_1} + \frac{1}{n_2}\right)} \tag{6.12}$$

$$\text{where } \sigma_{Pooled}^2 = \frac{(n_1 - 1)\widehat{\sigma_2^2} + (n_2 - 1)\widehat{\sigma_1^2}}{n_1 + n_2 - 2}.$$

Example 6.7

Obtain a 95% confidence interval for the difference in Microsoft stock prices between March 12 and March 30, 2012, and April 2 and April 21, 2012. The data is provided in Example 3.2.

Solution

Since the data belongs to the same company and are so close in time period, it is reasonable to assume that there is one variance for the company's stock prices and the two sample statistics are two estimates of the same population variance. Therefore, it is necessary to find their weighted averages and then use Equation 6.12. We already have the following results:

$$\widehat{\mu_1} = 32.32 \qquad \widehat{\sigma_1^2} = 0.10941$$

$$\widehat{\mu_2} = 31.27 \qquad \widehat{\sigma_2^2} = 0.372182$$

$$= t.inv(.025,15) = -2.144787$$

$$\sigma_{Pooled}^2 = \frac{(n_1 - 1)\widehat{\sigma_2^2} + (n_2 - 1)\widehat{\sigma_1^2}}{n_1 + n_2 - 2}$$

$$= \frac{(15-1)0.10941 + (15-1)0.372182}{15+15-2}$$

$$= \frac{1.531785 + 5.210554}{28} = 0.240798$$

$$LB = (\widehat{\mu_1} - \widehat{\mu_2}) \pm t_{a/2}\sqrt{\sigma_{Pooled}^2 \left(\frac{1}{n_1} + \frac{1}{n_2}\right)}$$

$$= (32.32 - 31.27) - 2.0484\sqrt{0.240798\left(\frac{1}{15} + \frac{1}{15}\right)}$$

$$= 1.05 - 2.0484\sqrt{0.032106} = 1.05 - 2.0484 \times 0.179183$$

(Continued)

$$= 1.05 - 0.3685$$

$$= 0.68$$

$$UB = (\widehat{\mu_1} - \widehat{\mu_2}) \pm t_{\alpha/2} \sqrt{\widehat{\sigma^2_{Pooled}} \left(\frac{1}{n_1} + \frac{1}{n_2} \right)}$$

$$= (32.32 - 31.27) + 2.0484 \sqrt{0.240798 \left(\frac{1}{15} + \frac{1}{15} \right)}$$

$$= 1.05 + 2.0484 \sqrt{0.032106} = 1.05 + 2.144787 \times 0.179183$$

$$= 1.05 + 0.3685$$

$$= 1.42$$

The range \$0.68 to \$1.42 covers the difference of the means of the two periods of stock prices for Microsoft with 95% probability.

The reason these results are exactly the same as the result for the previous case, where we did not assume the equality of the variances, is that the two sample sizes are equal. When samples have different sizes the results will be different.

Definition 6.8

Based on Chapter 5, the $(1 - \alpha)$% confidence interval for the **difference** of two **population proportions** $(\pi_1 - \pi_2)$ is given by the following equation:

$$(\widehat{\pi_1} - \widehat{\pi_2}) \pm Z_{\alpha/2} \sqrt{\frac{\widehat{\pi_1}(1 - \widehat{\pi_1})}{n_1} + \frac{\widehat{\pi_2}(1 - \widehat{\pi_2})}{n_2}} \qquad (6.13)$$

Example 6.8

Calculate a 95% confidence interval for the difference of the proportion of stock prices of Microsoft that are more than or equal to \$32.00 for the periods March 12–30, 2012, and April 2–21, 2012; the data is provided in Example 3.2.

(*Continued*)

(*Continued*)

Solution

Let's mark the data in March with the subscript "1" and those for April with subscript "2." The sample proportion of stocks more than or equal to $32.00 for each period is given by:

$$\widehat{\pi}_1 = \frac{13}{15} = 0.867 \qquad \widehat{\pi}_2 = \frac{3}{15} = 0.2$$

The Z value corresponding to 95% confidence is 1.96. Insert these values in Equation 6.13 to obtain the results.

$$LB = (0.867 - 0.2) - 1.96 \sqrt{\frac{0.867(1-0.867)}{15} + \frac{0.2(1-0.2)}{15}}$$

$$= 0.667 - 1.96 \times 0.1354$$
$$= 0.402$$

$$UB = (0.867 - 0.2) + 1.96 \sqrt{\frac{0.867(1-0.867)}{15} + \frac{0.2(1-0.2)}{15}}$$

$$= 0.667 + 1.96 \times 0.1354$$
$$= 0.933$$

The range from 0.402 to 0.933 covers the difference of the ratios of stock prices for Microsoft that is greater than or equal to $32.00 in the two periods March 12–30 and April 2–21.

Definition 6.9

Based on Chapter 5, the $(1-a)\%$ confidence interval for **one population variance** (σ^2) is given by the following equation:

$$\frac{(n-1)\widehat{\sigma}^2}{\chi^2_{a/2}} \le \sigma^2 \le \frac{(n-1)\widehat{\sigma}^2}{\chi^2_{1-a/2}} \tag{6.14}$$

Note that the chi-squared distribution is not symmetric, therefore we cannot use the ± signs to form the confidence interval. Also, it is important to note that the term $\chi^2_{a/2}$ refers to the right side of the distribution and, hence, it is larger than $\chi^2_{1-a/2}$, which refers to the left side of the distribution. Dividing the same numerator by a larger number provides a smaller result, hence the lower bond; while dividing the same numerator by a smaller value gives a larger result, hence the upper bond.

Example 6.9

Find the 95% confidence interval for the variance of stock prices for Microsoft. Use the sample data for the period April 2–21, 2012, provided in Example 3.2.

Solution

The sample variance for April 2–21 and the chi-squared values for 0.025 and 0.975 with 14 degrees of freedom are:

$$\widehat{\sigma^2} = 0.372182$$

$$\chi^{14}_{0.025} = 26.119$$

$$\chi^{14}_{0.925} = 5.629$$

Use Equation 6.14 to build the confidence interval

$$LB = \frac{(n-1)\widehat{\sigma^2}}{\chi^2_{a/2}} = \frac{(15-1)0.372182}{26.119} = 0.1995$$

$$UB = \frac{(n-1)\widehat{\sigma^2}}{\chi^2_{1-a/2}} = \frac{(15-1)0.372182}{5.629} = 0.9257$$

The range 0.1995 to 0.9257 covers the population variance of Microsoft stock prices with 95% confidence.

Definition 6.10

Based on Chapter 5, the $(1-a)\%$ confidence interval for the **ratio** of **two population variances** σ_1^2/σ_2^2 is given by the following equation:

$$\frac{\widehat{\sigma_1^2}/\widehat{\sigma_2^2}}{F_{1-a/2}} \leq \frac{\sigma_1^2}{\sigma_2^2} \leq \frac{\widehat{\sigma_1^2}/\widehat{\sigma_2^2}}{F_{a/2}} \tag{6.15}$$

Note that since the F distribution is not symmetric, we cannot use the $\pm$ signs to form the confidence interval. Also, it is important to note that term $F_{a/2}$ refers to the right side of the distribution and, hence, it is larger than $F_{1-a/2}$, which refers to the left side of the distribution. Dividing the same numerator by a larger number provides a smaller result, hence the lower bond, while dividing the same numerator by a smaller value gives a larger result, hence the upper bond.

Example 6.10

Find the confidence interval for the ratio of the variances for the two periods March 12–30, 2012, and April 2–21, 2012, for Microsoft stock prices.

Solution

Let's mark the data for March with the subscript "1" and those for April with subscript "2." The variances and the F values for 0.025 and 0.975 with 14 degrees of freedom are:

$$\sigma_1^2 = 0.10941$$

$$\sigma_2^2 = 0.372182$$

$$F_{0.025}^{14,14} = 2.891479$$

$$F_{0.925}^{14,14} = 0.339061$$

(Continued)

$$LB = \frac{\dfrac{0.372182}{0.10941}}{2.891479} = \frac{6.591466}{2.891479} = 2.28$$

$$UB = \frac{\dfrac{0.372182}{0.10941}}{0.339061} = \frac{6.591466}{0.339061} = 19.44035$$

The range 2.28 to 19.44035 covers the ratio of variances for the two periods for Microsoft stock prices with 95% confidence.

Since the confidence interval does not cover the value "1," it is unreasonable to believe that the variances of the two periods are the same. We will address this in more detail in Chapter 7, when we discuss the test of hypothesis. In light of this finding, we should use Equation 6.9 when testing equality of the means for the two periods, as in Example 6.6.

Determining the Sample Size

In Chapter 4 we showed the necessary sample size for estimating the single mean of a population. The sample size in that case was obtained by algebraic manipulation of the margin of error in Equation 6.4, which is repeated below for your reference.

$$\hat{\mu} \pm Z_{\alpha/2} \frac{\sigma}{\sqrt{n}} \tag{6.4}$$

Setting the margin of error equal to a desired margin of error, E, and solving for n results in the following formula:

$$\frac{\sigma^2 \left(Z_{\alpha/2}\right)^2}{E^2} \tag{6.16}$$

Example 6.11

What size sample is needed to be within $0.10 of the actual price if the variance is 0.372182 with 95% confidence?

Solution

$$n = \frac{0.372182 \times 1.96^2}{0.1^2} = 142.98$$

Therefore, the necessary sample size is 143. Note that the variance in this formula is the population variance. When the population variance is unknown, use the sample variance instead, but remember to use the t value instead of the Z value.

Similar algebraic manipulations are applied to obtain sample sizes for cases with unknown variances, involving, both, the one or two population means, proportions, and variances. We will only show the results for one population proportions for reference.

$$n = \frac{\hat{\pi}(1 - \hat{\pi})\left(Z_{\alpha/2}\right)^2}{E^2} \tag{6.17}$$

Example 6.11

What size sample is needed to be within 5% of the population proportion with 95% confidence when the sample proportion is 0.4?

Solution

$$n = \frac{(0.4 \times 0.6)1.96}{0.05^2} = 372.182$$

Therefore, the necessary sample size is $n = 369$.

Inference with Confidence Intervals

The primary objective of statistics is to make inferences about population parameters using sample statistics. Using sample statistics to make deductions about population parameters is called statistical inference. Statistical inference can be based on point estimation, confidence interval, or test of hypothesis. These are closely related and in some aspects they are interchangeable. The inference can be based on the estimation theory or decision theory. Test of hypothesis is a tool for decision theory. The estimation theory consists of point estimation and interval estimation. This section will deal with the **confidence interval**.

Population parameters are unknown and constants. Sample statistics, which are random by nature, are used to provide estimates of population parameters. If sampling is random, then the sample statistics is a good estimate of the corresponding population parameter. A good sample statistics has desirable properties, as discussed in Chapter 3. These statistics are called point estimates because they

Table 6.1. Summary of Confidence Interval for One Population Parameter

Parameter	Statistics	Distribution	Variance	Confidence interval
μ	$\hat{\mu}$	Normal	Known	$\hat{\mu} \pm Z_{\alpha/2} \dfrac{\sigma}{\sqrt{n}}$
			Unknown	$\hat{\mu} \pm t_{\alpha/2} \dfrac{\hat{\sigma}}{\sqrt{n}}$
		Unknown	Known	$\hat{\mu} \pm t_{\alpha/2} \dfrac{\hat{\sigma}}{\sqrt{n}}$
			Unknown	$\hat{\mu} \pm t_{\alpha/2} \dfrac{\hat{\sigma}}{\sqrt{n}}$
π	$\hat{\pi}$	Normal or Unknown	Always Known	$\hat{\pi} \pm Z_{\alpha/2} \sqrt{\dfrac{\hat{\pi}(1-\hat{\pi})}{n}}$
σ^2	$\widehat{\sigma^2}$	Normal	Always Unknown	$\dfrac{(n-1)\widehat{\sigma^2}}{\chi^2_{\alpha/2}} \leq \sigma^2 \leq \dfrac{(n-1)\widehat{\sigma^2}}{\chi^2_{1-\alpha/2}}$

Table 6.2. *Confidence Interval for Two Samples*

Parameter	Statistic	Status of variances	Confidence interval
$\mu_1 - \mu_2$	$\widehat{\mu}_1 - \widehat{\mu}_2$	Known and Unequal	$\widehat{\mu}_1 - \widehat{\mu}_2 \pm Z_{\alpha/2}\sqrt{\dfrac{\sigma_1^2}{n_1} + \dfrac{\sigma_2^2}{n_1}}$
		Known and Equal	$(\widehat{\mu}_1 - \widehat{\mu}_2) \pm Z_{\alpha/2}\sqrt{\sigma^2\left(\dfrac{1}{n_1} + \dfrac{1}{n_2}\right)}$
		Unknown and Unequal	$(\widehat{\mu}_1 - \widehat{\mu}_2) \pm t_{\alpha/2}\sqrt{\dfrac{\widehat{\sigma_1^2}}{n_1} + \dfrac{\widehat{\sigma_2^2}}{n_2}}$
		Unknown and Equal	$(\widehat{\mu}_1 - \widehat{\mu}_2) \pm t_{\alpha/2}\sqrt{\widehat{\sigma_{Pooled}^2}\left(\dfrac{1}{n_1} + \dfrac{1}{n_2}\right)}$
$\pi_1 - \pi_2$	$\widehat{\pi}_1 - \widehat{\pi}_2$	Always Unknown	$(\widehat{\pi}_1 - \widehat{\pi}_2) \pm Z_{\alpha/2}\sqrt{\dfrac{\widehat{\pi}_1(1-\widehat{\pi}_1)}{n_1} + \dfrac{\widehat{\pi}_2(1-\widehat{\pi}_2)}{n_2}}$
$\dfrac{\sigma_1^2}{\sigma_2^2}$	$\widehat{\sigma_1^2}\Big/\widehat{\sigma_2^2}$	Always Unknown	$\dfrac{\widehat{\sigma_1^2}\big/\widehat{\sigma_2^2}}{F_{1-\alpha/2}} \leq \dfrac{\sigma_1^2}{\sigma_2^2} \leq \dfrac{\widehat{\sigma_1^2}\big/\widehat{\sigma_2^2}}{F_{\alpha/2}}$

provide a single value as the estimate of the population parameter. If the estimator is "good" then it should be close to the unknown true value of the population parameter. The single estimate does not indicate proximity to the true parameter or probability of being close to the true parameter. Confidence intervals give, both, an idea of actual value of population parameter and also a probability, or a level of confidence, that the interval includes the population parameter.

CHAPTER 7

Statistical Inference with Test of Hypothesis

Choose Evidence with High Probability

One of the methods of drawing inference about population parameters using sample statistics is by testing the hypothesis about the parameters. With proper sampling techniques, a point estimate provides the best estimate of the population parameter. Interval estimation provides a desired level of probability of level of confidence in the estimate. Test of hypothesis is used to make assertions on whether a hypothesized parameter can be refuted based on evidence from a sample.

Using sample statistics to make deductions about population parameters is called statistical inference. Statistical inference can be based on point estimation, confidence interval, or test of hypothesis. They are closely related and in some aspects they are interchangeable. This section will deal with test of hypothesis. The technical definition of a hypothesis is based on the distributional properties of random variables.

The purpose of test of hypothesis is to make a decision on the validity of the value of a parameter stated in the null hypothesis based on the observed sample statistics. Recall that **parameters** are **constant** and **unknown** while **statistics** are **variable** and **known**. You calculate and observe the statistics. If the observed statistics is reasonably close to the hypothesized value, then nothing unexpected has happened and the (minor) difference can be attributed to **random error**. If the observed statistics is too far away from the hypothesized value, then either the null hypothesis is true and something unusual with very low probability happened, or the null hypothesis is false and the sample consists of **unusual** observations. Following sampling procedures and obtaining a random sample reduces the chance of an unusual sample, which may still occur in rare occasions. Therefore, proper sampling assures that unusual sample statistics have low probabilities. On the other hand, sample statistics representing the more common possibilities would have a high probability of being selected.

Statistical inference consists of accepting outcomes with high probability and rejecting outcomes with low probability. If the sample statistics does not contradict the hypothesized parameter, then the hypothesized parameter should not be rejected. If the probability of observed statistics is low we reject the null hypothesis; otherwise we fail to reject the null hypothesis. In order to find the probability of an occurrence for sample statistics we need to know its sampling distribution.

Hypothesis

A hypothesis is formed to make a statement about a parameter. Although in English language terms such as "statement" and "claim" may be used interchangeably, in statistics, as will be explained shortly, we use the word "claim" only about the alternative hypothesis.

Definition 7.1

A **statistical hypothesis** is an assertion about the distribution of one or more random variables. When a hypothesis completely specifies the distribution, it is called a **simple** statistical hypothesis; otherwise, it is called a **composite** statistical hypothesis.

Hypotheses are customarily expressed in terms of parameters of the corresponding distribution function. If the parameter is set equal to a specific value it is a simple hypothesis; otherwise it is a composite hypothesis. For example, the hypothesis that the average price of a particular stock is $33.69 is written as $\mu = 33.69$. This is a **simple hypothesis**. However, the hypothesis that the average price of a particular stock is less than $33.69 is written as $\mu < 33.69$. This is a composite hypothesis because it **does not completely specify** the distribution.

Definition 7.2

When the hypothesis gives **an exact value** for all unknown parameters of the assumed distribution function, it is called a **simple hypothesis**; otherwise the hypothesis is composite.

In this text we deal with the simple hypothesis exclusively.

Null Hypothesis

The null hypothesis reflects the status quo. It is about **how things have been** or **are currently**. For example, the average life of a car is 7 years. The null hypothesis can be a statement about the **nature of something**, such as, "an average man is 5'10" tall." The null hypothesis might be the **deliberate setting of equipment**, such as, "a soda-dispensing machine puts 12 ounces of liquid in a can." A statistical hypothesis is not limited to the average only. We can have a hypothesis about any **parameter** of a distribution function, such as, 54% of adults are Democrats; the variance for weekly sales is 50. The symbol for a null hypothesis is $\mathbf{H_0}$, pronounced **h-sub-zero**. The following represent the previous examples in the customary notation of the hypothesis. Note that the stated null hypotheses are **simple hypotheses** as we will only address tests of simple hypotheses.

Single Mean

$H_0: \mu = 7$

$H_0: \mu = 5'10"$

$H_0: \mu = 12$

Single Proportion

$H_0: \pi = 0.54$

Single Variance

$H_0: \sigma^2 = 50$

In summary, the **null hypothesis** is a **fact of life, the way things have been, or a state of nature**. This includes the setting of machinery, or deliberate calibration of equipment. If the fact of life, the state of nature, the setting of machinery, the calibration of equipment has not changed, or there is no doubt about them, then the null hypothesis is not tested. When you purchase a can of soda that states it contains 12 ounces of drink you do not check to see if it does actually contain 12 ounces; you have no doubt about it, so you do not test it. Many such "null hypotheses" are believed to be true and, hence, not tested. It is tempting to state that the manufacturer is making the "claim" that the can contains 12 ounces; however, their statement is more of an assertion or a promise and not a claim. As we will see shortly, the alternative hypothesis is the **claim** of the researcher, which is also known as the **research question**. The null hypothesis for a simple hypothesis is always equal to a constant. The format is:

$$H_0: \text{A parameter} = \text{A constant} \qquad (7.1)$$

In order to test a hypothesis, we either have to know the distribution function or the random variables. If the distribution function has more than one parameter, we need to know the other parameter(s); otherwise we will be dealing with a composite hypothesis.

In a hypothesis, testing the **expected value** of the outcome of an experiment is the hypothesized value. The hypothesized value reflects the status quo and will prevail until rejected. In practice, the observed value is indeed a **statistics** obtained from a sample of reasonable size. Care must be taken.

When testing a hypothesis about variance, note that the constant (σ_0^2) should be a non-negative number. In practice, zero variance is not a reasonable choice and the value is usually positive. This parameter is different than the mean or proportion, and it has a chi-squared distribution. Therefore, its test statistics will be very different from the others.

Null Hypothesis for Equality of Two Parameters

The test of hypothesis can be used to test the equality of parameters from two populations. Let θ_1 and θ_2 be two parameters from two populations. With no prior information the two parameters would be assumed to be the same until proven otherwise. For example, the average productivity of a man and a woman would be the same until proven otherwise. The null hypothesis should not be written as:

$$H_0: \theta_1 = \theta_2 \tag{7.2}$$

This hypothesis is setting one parameter equal to the other, which makes it a composite hypothesis. Using algebra the hypothesis can be modified to convert it to a simple hypothesis. There are two possible modifications. Equation (7.2) can be written in the following two forms.

$$H_0: \theta_1 - \theta_2 = 0, \text{ or} \tag{7.3}$$

$$H_0: \frac{\theta_1}{\theta_2} = 1 \tag{7.4}$$

The only thing that remains to be established is that the difference of two parameters or the ratio of two parameters is also a parameter, and that we have an appropriate distribution function to use as test statistics. We have accomplished these in Chapter 5, but will reinforce them in this chapter as well.

Null Hypothesis of Two Means

The representations in Equations 7.3 and 7.4 are to test the equality of two parameters. Depending on the parameters, we may use one or the other representation based on availability of a distribution function. In Chapter 5, we showed appropriate distribution functions for the **difference of two means** of random variables, each with a normal distribution. The difference of two means from a normally distributed function is a parameter, and if the two are equal, their difference will be zero. This will allow the use of normal distribution for testing the following hypothesis, which is identical to $H_0: \mu_1 = \mu_2$.

$$H_0: \mu_1 - \mu_2 = 0 \tag{7.5}$$

Null Hypothesis of Two Proportions

In Chapter 5, we showed that if a population has a normal distribution with proportion π_1 and another population has a normal distribution with proportion π_2, the difference of the two parameters will also have a normal distribution with the proportion $\pi_1 - \pi_2$. The difference of the two proportions of two normal populations is a parameter, and if the two are equal, their difference will be zero. This will allow the use of normal distribution for testing the following hypothesis, which is identical to $H_0: \pi_1 = \pi_2$.

$$H_0: \pi_1 - \pi_2 = 0 \qquad\qquad (7.6)$$

Null Hypothesis of Two Variances σ_1^2

In Chapter 5, we showed that σ^2 has a chi-squared distribution. The ratio of σ_1^2 to σ_2^2, after each is divided by its degrees of freedom, has an F distribution (see Chapter 5). The F distribution will have degrees of freedom associated with the corresponding numerator and denominator chi-squared distributions. The ratio of two variances is a parameter with F distribution, and if they are equal then their ratio will be equal to 1. This will allow the use of F distribution for testing the following hypothesis, which is identical to $H_0: \sigma_1^2 = \sigma_2^2$.

$$H_0: \frac{\sigma_1^2}{\sigma_2^2} = 1 \qquad\qquad (7.7)$$

Alternative Hypothesis

The alternative hypothesis is the **claim** a researcher has against the null hypothesis. It is the research question or the main purpose of the research. The formation of the null and the alternative hypotheses are the main problem of the novice. Remember the following:

- The null hypothesis is always of this form:
  A parameter = A constant when we deal with simple hypothesis.
  All of the previous null hypotheses are simple hypothesis.

- The claim might be that the parameter is greater than (>), less than (<), or not equal to (≠) a constant, which reflects the claim that the parameter has increased (>), decreased (<), or it simply has changed (≠).
- Null means something that nullifies something else. Therefore, the null hypothesis is the value that nullifies the alternative hypothesis. In all three cases the relationship that nullifies the (>), (<), and (≠) is the (=) sign.

The alternative hypothesis is designated by H_1 and is pronounced **h-sub-one** or **alternative hypothesis**. The only time a hypothesis is formed and consequently tested is when there is a doubt about null hypothesis.

How to Determine the Alternative Hypothesis

The claim of the research, that is, the research question, determines the alternative hypothesis. Every alternative hypothesis is a claim that the null hypothesis has changed. When the claim is that the value of parameter in the null hypothesis has declined, then the appropriate sign is the "**less than**" sign (<). Focus on the meaning and not the wording. When the claim is that the value of the parameter in the null hypothesis has increased, then the appropriate sign is the "**greater than**" sign (>). These two alternative hypotheses are known as **one-tailed hypotheses**. When the claim is not specific, or is indeterminate, then the appropriate sign is the "not equal" sign (≠). This is known as a **two-tailed hypothesis**. None of the three alternative cases include an equal sign (=), because the equal sign nullifies all of the above signs. Furthermore, in order to draw inference at this introductory level, the null hypothesis must be a simple hypothesis, which takes the form H_0: A parameter = A constant.

Alternative Hypothesis for a Single Mean

- A consumer advocacy group claims that car manufacturers are cutting corners to maintain profitability and make inferior cars that do not last as long.

  $H_0: \mu = 7$

  $H_1: \mu < 7$

- Men are getting taller because of better nutrition and more exercise.

  $H_0: \mu = 5'10"$

  $H_1: \mu > 5'10"$

- The quality manager would like to know if the calibration of soda dispensing machine is still correct.

  $H_0: \mu = 12$

  $H_1: \mu \neq 12$

Alternative Hypothesis for a Single Proportion

- A political science researcher believes that due to globalization of the economy and political turmoil around the world, the percentage of Democrats has declined.

  $H_0: \pi = 0.54$

  $H_1: \pi < 0.54$

Alternative Hypothesis for a Single Variance

- Increased promotional advertising has increased the variance of weekly sales.

  $H_0: \sigma^2 = 50$

  $H_1: \sigma^2 > 50$

The alternative hypothesis is the claim someone has against the status quo. If there is no claim, then there is no alternative hypothesis and, hence, no need for a test. The nature of the claim determines the sign of the alternative. In the alternative hypothesis the parameter under consideration can be less than, greater than, or not equal to the constant stated in the null hypothesis. The sign of the alternative hypothesis depends on the claim and nothing else.

Test Statistics

In Chapter 5 we saw that when statistics is a sample mean ($\hat{\mu}$), a sample proportion ($\hat{\pi}$), two sample means ($\widehat{\mu_1} - \widehat{\mu_2}$), or two sample proportions ($\widehat{\pi_1} - \widehat{\pi_2}$), the Central Limit Theorem asserts that each of these sample

Table 7.1. Summary of Null and Alternative Hypothesis

Case	Null hypothesis	Alternative hypothesis	Comments
Single Mean	μ = A constant	μ > A constant μ < A constant $\mu \neq$ A constant	The claim determines the sign of the alternative hypothesis.
Single Proportion	π = A constant	π > A constant π < A constant $\pi \neq$ A constant	The claim determines the sign of the alternative hypothesis.
Single Variance	σ^2 = A constant	σ^2 > A constant σ^2 < A constant $\sigma^2 \neq$ A constant	The claim determines the sign of the alternative hypothesis.
Two Means	$\mu_1 - \mu_2$ = A constant	$\mu_1 - \mu_2$ > A constant $\mu_1 - \mu_2$ < A constant $\mu_1 - \mu_2 \neq$ A constant	Use to test the equality of two means.
Two Proportions	$\pi_1 - \pi_2$ = A constant	$\pi_1 - \pi_2$ > A constant $\pi_1 - \pi_2$ < A constant $\pi_1 - \pi_2 \neq$ A constant	Use to test the equality of two proportions.
Two Variances	$\dfrac{\sigma_1^2}{\sigma_2^2}$ = A constant	$\dfrac{\sigma_1^2}{\sigma_2^2}$ > A constant	Use to test the equality of variances. Usually, no other alternative is tested.

statistics have a normal distribution. Sample variance $(\widehat{\sigma^2})$ has a chi-squared distribution. The ratio of two sample variances $\left(\widehat{\sigma_1^2} \big/ \widehat{\sigma_2^2}\right)$ has an F distribution. Cases involving two statistics test their equality. The test statistics for single mean (μ), two means ($\mu_1 - \mu_2$), single proportion (π), and two proportions ($\pi_1 - \pi_2$) is provided by

$$\text{Test statistics} = \frac{\text{Observed} - \text{Expected}}{\text{Standard deviation of observed}} \qquad (7.8)$$

The statistics obtained from the sample provides the **observed** portion of the formula. The null hypothesis provides the **expected** value. The other name for **standard deviation of the observed value** is **standard error**. The **Central Limit Theorem** provides the distribution function and the standard error. The sampling distribution of sample statistics covered in Chapter 5 provides a summary of parameters, statistics, and sampling variances of one and two populations. Whether the correct statistics for this hypothesis is Z test or t test depends on whether the population variance is known. Use the Z test when the population variance is known, or when it is unknown and sample size is large. Note that Z statistics can only be used to test hypothesis about one mean, one proportion, two means, or two proportions. In the case of two means or two proportions, the hypotheses must be modified to resemble a **simple hypothesis**. Use t statistics when the population variance is unknown and sample size is small. Note that t statistics can only be used to test hypotheses about one mean, one proportion, two means, or two proportions.

The test statistics for a single variance (σ^2) is given by

$$\chi^2 = \frac{(n-1)\widehat{\sigma^2}}{\sigma_0^2} \tag{7.9}$$

The test statistics for equality of two variances $\left(\sigma_1^2 / \sigma_2^2\right)$ is given by

$$F = \frac{\widehat{\sigma_1^2}}{\widehat{\sigma_2^2}} \tag{7.10}$$

The actual tests are provided in Table 7.2, which is a summary of tools developed in Chapters 5, 6, and 7.

All the null hypotheses are set **equal to a constant**. In the case of equality of two means and two proportions, the constant is **zero**. In the case of equality of two variances, the constant is **one**. Subscript zero represents the hypothesized null value, which is a constant.

Statistical Inference

Everything in this chapter up to this point was in preparation for conducting statistical inferences. There are two approaches for testing a hypothesis. The first one is the method of P value and the second is the method of critical region. The two approaches are similar, but first we need to explain the concept of inferential statistics.

Any event that has a probability of occurrence will occur. Some events have higher probability of occurrence than others, so they will

Table 7.2. Test Statistics for Testing Hypotheses

Case	Null hypothesis	Variance	Test statistics
Single Mean	μ	Known	$Z = \dfrac{\hat{\mu} - \mu_0}{\dfrac{\hat{\sigma}}{\sqrt{n}}}$
		Unknown	$t = \dfrac{\hat{\mu} - \mu_0}{\dfrac{\hat{\sigma}}{\sqrt{n}}}$
Single Proportion	π	Unknown	$Z = \dfrac{\hat{\pi} - \pi_0}{\sqrt{\dfrac{\pi_0(1 - \pi_0)}{n}}}$
Single Variance	σ^2	Unknown	$\chi = \dfrac{(n-1)\widehat{\sigma^2}}{\sigma_0^2}$
Two Means	$\mu_1 - \mu_2$	Known and Unequal	$Z = \dfrac{\left(\widehat{\mu_1} - \widehat{\mu_2}\right) - (\mu_1 - \mu_2)}{\sqrt{\dfrac{\sigma_1^2}{n_1} + \dfrac{\sigma_2^2}{n_2}}}$
		Known and Equal	$Z = \dfrac{\left(\widehat{\mu_1} - \widehat{\mu_2}\right) - (\mu_1 - \mu_2)}{\sqrt{\sigma^2\dfrac{1}{n_1} + \dfrac{1}{n_2}}}$
		Unknown and Unequal	$t = \dfrac{\left(\widehat{\mu_1} - \widehat{\mu_2}\right) - (\mu_1 - \mu_2)}{\sqrt{\dfrac{\widehat{\sigma_1^2}}{n_1} + \dfrac{\widehat{\sigma_2^2}}{n_2}}}$
		Unknown and Equal	$t = \dfrac{\left(\widehat{\mu_1} - \widehat{\mu_2}\right) - (\mu_1 - \mu_2)}{\sqrt{\widehat{\sigma_{Pooled}^2}\dfrac{1}{n_1} + \dfrac{1}{n_2}}}$
Two Proportions	$\pi_1 - \pi_2$	Unknown	$Z = \dfrac{\left(\widehat{\pi_1} - \widehat{\pi_2}\right) - (\pi_1 - \pi_2)}{\sqrt{\dfrac{\pi_1(1 - \pi_1)}{n_1} + \dfrac{\pi_2(1 - \pi_2)}{n_2}}}$
Two Variances	$\dfrac{\sigma_1^2}{\sigma_2^2}$	Unknown	$F = \dfrac{\widehat{\sigma_1^2}}{\widehat{\sigma_2^2}}$

occur more often. The essence of statistical inference is that events that have high probability of occurrence are assumed to occur while events with low probability of occurrence are assumed not to occur. To clarify, take the probability of having an accident while going through an intersection. The probability of having an accident crossing an intersection when the traffic light is green is much lower than the probability of having an accident crossing the intersection when the traffic light is red. The statistical inference in this case would be that the chance of having an accident while crossing an intersection when the light is green is negligible, so we should go through an intersection when the light is green. On the other hand, the probability of having an accident when the light is red is high so we should not go through a red light. Note that there is still a chance that you go through a green light at an intersection and have an accident. It is also possible to go through a red light without having an accident. These possibilities have low probabilities, so we "**assume**" they will not occur. This example has a special twist to it. Note that for every car involved in an accident while crossing an intersection when the light was green, the other party to the accident must have gone through a red light. The null and alternative hypothesis can be expressed as

H_0: Going through green light does NOT cause an accident;
H_1: Going through green light does cause an accident.

Note that the null hypothesis here is not a simple hypothesis because it is not of the form:

A Parameter = A Constant

Therefore, this hypothesis cannot be tested by Z or t statistics, at least in its present form. However, it is sufficient to explain the concept.

Types of Error

The process of testing a hypothesis is similar to convicting a criminal. The **null hypothesis** is a conjecture to the effect that everybody is assumed to be innocent unless proven otherwise. If there is any reason to doubt this innocence, a **claim** is made against the **null hypothesis**, which is called an alternative hypothesis. The type of crime is decided, as indicated by charges of misdemeanor, felony, and so forth, which is similar to test statistics. Within this domain the evidence is collected, which is the same as taking a **sample**. Finally, based on the evidence a judgment is made, either innocent or guilty. If the prosecutor fails to provide evidence that the person is guilty, it does not mean that the person is innocent. The degree or the probability that the person was innocent (but was convicted) is the probability of type I error, or the *P value*.

We start by assuming the null hypothesis that the suspect is innocent. We calculate a test statistics using the null hypothesis. This is similar to presenting evidence in the legal system assuming the suspect is innocent. Then the test statistics is compared to the norm, provided by the appropriate statistical table. The null hypothesis of innocence is rejected if the probability of being innocent is low in light of evidence. Otherwise, we fail to reject the null hypothesis. Suppose we had a case that the probability was low enough and we actually rejected the null hypothesis. The basis for rejecting the null was low probability, but the observed statistics was nevertheless possible. It is possible that the null hypothesis is true, a sample statistics with low probability was observed, and we erroneously rejected the null hypothesis. This kind of error is known as type I error.

Definition 7.3

Type I Error occurs when the null hypothesis is true but is rejected.

Definition 7.4

Type II Error occurs when the null hypothesis was false but was not rejected.

It is not possible to commit type I error if the null hypothesis is not rejected. It is not possible to commit type II error if the null hypothesis is rejected. There is a **type III error**, which will be discussed shortly.

Definition 7.5

Type III error is rejecting a null hypothesis in favor of an alternative hypothesis with the wrong sign.

Table 7.3. *Summary of Types of Error in Inference*

	H_0 **Rejected**	H_0 **Not rejected**
H_0 is True	Type I Error	No Error
H_1 is True	No Error	Type II Error

Statistical Inference with the Method of P value

The observed value of sample statistics, such as sample mean and sample proportion, can be converted to a standardized value such as Z or t. Under null hypothesis, observed statistics should be **close to** the corresponding population parameter. This means that the corresponding standardized value should be **close to zero**. Recall that the numerators of Z and t are the difference between sample statistics and population parameter, which is also called individual error. The further the calculated statistics is from the parameter, the larger the value of the standardized sample statistics is. In other words, the test statistics become larger when the observed statistics is further from the hypothesized parameter. The area under the curve from the value of the test statistics reflects the probability of observing that or a more extreme value if the null hypothesis is correct. This probability, reflecting the **area under the tail area** of the normal or t distribution, reflects the probability of observing a **more extreme value** than the observed statistics. The smaller this probability is, the less likely that the null hypothesis is correct. Recall that in statistics, as in real life, we assume that events that are not likely will not occur, which is the same as saying that events that occur are more likely. Therefore, the statistics that is observed from a random sample must be more likely to occur than other events. The area under the tail area corresponding to the extreme values actually represents the likelihood of the event.

Definition 7.6

The value representing the probability of the area under the tail-end of the distribution is called the p **value**. This gives rise to the following rule for statistical inference.

Rule 7.1

Reject the null hypothesis when the p value is **small enough**.

Since it is possible that the unlikely event has occurred, the above rule will always be wrong when the sample statistics is the result of a rare sample outcome. Thus, in such cases, rejecting the null hypothesis will result in **type I error**. Fortunately, by definition, this erroneous conclusion will seldom happen. The exact probability of committing such a type I error is actually equal to the area under the tail-end of the distribution.

Definition 7.7

The **P value** is equal to the probability of **type I error**. It is also called the **Observed Significant Level (OSL)**.

Type I error can only occur if we reject the null hypothesis. This might lead to the decision to make type I error very small, but not rejecting the null hypothesis unless the p value, that is, the probability of type I error, is very small. The problem with this strategy is that it increases the probability of not rejecting the null hypothesis when it is false, which means the probability of **type II** increases. There is a tradeoff between type I and type II errors: decreasing one increases the other. The tradeoff is not linear, which is the same as saying that they do not add up to one. The only possible way to reduce both type I and type II error is by increasing the sample size.

Significance level indicates the probability or likelihood that observed results could have happened by chance, given that the null hypothesis is true. If the null hypothesis is true, observed results should have high probability. Consequently, when p value is high, there is no reason to doubt that the null hypothesis is true. However, if the observed results happen to have a low probability, it casts doubt about the validity of the null hypothesis because we expect high probability events to occur. Since the outcome has occurred by virtue of being observed, they imply that the null hypothesis is not likely to be true. In other words, p value is the probability of seeing what you saw, which is reflected in the other common name for p value, OSL.

Statistical Inference with Method of Critical Region

An alternative approach to the decision rule of P value is to calculate a **critical value** and compare the test statistics to it. In order to obtain a critical value, decide on the level of type I error you are willing and able to commit, for example 2.5%. Look up that probability in the body of the table such as a table for normal distribution. Read the corresponding

Z score from the margins. **The Z score corresponding to the chosen level of type I error is the critical value.**

Rule 7.2

Reject the null hypothesis when the test statistics is more extreme than the critical value.

As long as the same level of type I error is selected, the two methods result in the same conclusion. The method of *P value* is preferred because it gives the exact probability of type I error, while in the method of critical region the probability of type I error is never exact. If the test statistics is more extreme than the critical value, the probability of type I error is less than the selected probability. Another advantage of *P value* is that it allows the researcher to make a more informed decision.

Steps for Test of Hypothesis

1. Determine the scope of the test
2. State the null hypothesis
3. Determine the alternative hypothesis
4. Determine a suitable test statistics
5. Calculate the test statistics
6. Provide inference

Test of Hypothesis with Confidence Interval

We covered confidence intervals in Chapter 6 when discussing estimation. Confidence intervals can be used to test a two-tailed hypothesis. Proceed to calculate the confidence interval based on the desired level of significance, as shown in Chapter 6, and apply the following rule to draw inference.

Rule 7.3

Reject the null hypothesis when the confidence interval does NOT cover the hypothesized value. Fail to reject when the confidence interval does cover the hypothesized value.

Whether the confidence interval is for one parameter or two does not matter. Rule 7.3 applies to all confidence intervals regardless of the parameter. So it can be used for a two tailed test of hypothesis of one or two parameter confidence interval for means, percentages, or variances. The approach is based on the critical region method.

The coverage of the test of hypothesis completes the set of tools needed for making inferences. We now provide examples for tests of hypotheses for one mean, one proportion, and one variance. Then we give examples for tests of hypotheses for the equality of two means, two proportions, and two variances.

Since we will be using the stock price data, we have reproduced the same data for your convenience.

Date	WMT	MSFT	Date	WMT	MSFT
12 Mar.	$60.68	$32.04	2 Apr.	$61.36	$32.29
13 Mar.	$61.00	$32.67	3 Apr.	$60.65	$31.94
14 Mar.	$61.08	$32.77	4 Apr.	$60.26	$31.21
15 Mar.	$61.23	$32.85	5 Apr.	$60.67	$31.52
16 Mar.	$60.84	$32.60	9 Apr.	$60.13	$31.10
19 Mar.	$60.74	$32.20	10 Apr.	$59.93	$30.47
20 Mar.	$60.60	$31.99	11 Apr.	$59.80	$30.35
21 Mar.	$60.56	$31.91	12 Apr.	$60.14	$30.98
22 Mar.	$60.65	$32.00	13 Apr.	$59.77	$30.81
23 Mar.	$60.75	$32.01	16 Apr.	$60.58	$31.08
26 Mar.	$61.20	$32.59	17 Apr.	$61.87	$31.44
27 Mar.	$61.09	$32.52	18 Apr.	$62.06	$31.14
28 Mar.	$61.19	$32.19	19 Apr.	$61.75	$31.01
29 Mar.	$60.82	$32.12	20 Apr.	$62.45	$32.42
30 Mar.	$61.20	$32.26	21 Apr.	$59.54	$32.12
Mean	$60.89	$32.32		$60.82	$31.27
Variance	0.056464	0.109413		0.826873	0.372182
St. Dev	$0.24	0.330777		0.909325	$0.61

The point estimates at the bottom of the table are calculated using Excel, some of which are off by a small margin.

Example 7.1

An investor would purchase Microsoft stock if the average price exceeded $32.00. Using the data from March 12 to March 30, would he buy the stock?

Solution

Based on the statement in the problem the alternative hypothesis is:

$$H_1: \mu > 32 \quad \Rightarrow \quad H_0: \mu = 32$$

From previous examples we have the following statistics that are obtained from Excel.

$$\hat{\mu} = 32.32 \qquad \widehat{\sigma^2} = 0.1094$$

Since population variance is unknown we need to use

$$t = \frac{\hat{\mu} - \mu_0}{\frac{\hat{\sigma}}{\sqrt{n}}} = \frac{32.32 - 32}{\sqrt{\frac{0.1094}{15}}} = \frac{0.32}{0.085401} = 3.747028$$

Using the following Excel command we obtain the exact *P value*.

$$= t.dist.rt(3.747028,14) = 0.001083$$

The probability of obtaining an average of $32.32, if the true population average is $32.00, is only 0.001083. This is a low probability. Therefore, we reject the null hypothesis in favor of the alternative hypothesis. Alternatively, we could say that the probability of type I error, if we reject the null hypothesis, is only 0.001083 and hence, we reject the null hypothesis. If you copy the value of the "*t*" into the formula for the *P value* you will get the same number as shown above, that is 0.001083. However, if you type in the rounded number, which is "3.74," you would get "0.001098." The first number is more accurate because it uses the precise answer for "*t*."

Example 7.2

Test the claim that more than 50% of the stock prices for Microsoft close higher than \$32.20. Use the sample from March 12 to March 30, 2012.

Solution

Sorting the data makes it easier to obtain the portion of sample prices over \$32.20.

$$\hat{\pi} = \frac{8}{15} = 0.53$$

Based on the statement in the problem the alternative hypothesis is:

$$H_1: \pi > 0.50 \quad \Rightarrow \quad H_0: \pi = 0.5$$

From Table 7.2 the correct formula is:

$$Z = \frac{\hat{\pi} - \pi_0}{\sqrt{\dfrac{\pi_0(1 - \pi_0)}{n}}} = \frac{0.53 - 0.50}{\sqrt{\dfrac{0.50 \times 0.50}{15}}} = \frac{0.03}{0.13} = 0.23$$

The probability of the region more extreme than $Z = 0.23$ is given by

$$P(Z > 0.23) = 0.5 - P(0 < Z < 0.23) = 0.5 - 0.0910 = 0.4090$$

Since the probability of type I error, if we reject the null hypothesis, is too high, we fail to reject the null hypothesis.

Example 7.3

Test the claim that the variance for the stock prices of Microsoft is greater than 0.9. Use the sample from March 12 to March 30, 2012.

Solution

Based on the statement in the problem the alternative hypothesis is:

$$H_0: \sigma^2 > 0.90 \quad \Rightarrow \quad H_1: \sigma^2 = 0.90$$

(*Continued*)

(*Continued*)

From Table 7.2 the appropriate formula is:

$$\chi = \frac{(n-1)\widehat{\sigma}^2}{\sigma_0^2} = \frac{(15-1)(0.10941)}{0.90} = \frac{1.531785}{0.90} = 1.702$$

Using the following Excel command we obtain the *P value*:

$$= \text{chisq.dist.rt}(1.702,14) = 0.99997$$

Since the probability of type I error is too high, we fail to reject the null hypothesis.

Example 7.4

Are the means for Microsoft stock prices for periods March 12–30 and April 2–21 the same?

Solution

The objective is to determine if $\mu_1 = \mu_2$. Since this format is not of the form of a parameter equal to a constant, we rewrite the hypothesis as:

$$H_0: \mu_1 - \mu_2 = 0 \qquad H_1: \mu_1 - \mu_2 \neq 0$$

Since no particular directional claim has been made, the test is a two-tailed test. The following information is available:

$$\widehat{\mu_1} = 32.32 \qquad \widehat{\mu_2} = 32.27$$
$$\sigma_1^2 = 0.10941 \qquad \sigma_2^2 = 0.372182$$

Since we do not know whether the variances are equal, we will test their equality first, that is, $\sigma_1^2 = \sigma_2^2$. Since this is of the form of a parameter equal to another parameter, it has to be modified to resemble a parameter = a constant format.

(*Continued*)

$$H_0: \frac{\sigma_1^2}{\sigma_2^2} = 1 \qquad H_1: \frac{\sigma_1^2}{\sigma_2^2} > 1$$

It is customary to express this alternative hypothesis in the "greater than one" format. To assure that the ratio of the sample variances is actually greater than one, always place the sample variance that is larger in the numerator.

From Table 7.2, the appropriate formula to test the equality of two variances is

$$F = \frac{\widehat{\sigma_1^2}}{\widehat{\sigma_2^2}} = \frac{0.372182}{0.10941} = 3.4017$$

The P value for this statistic is obtained from the following Excel command:

$$= \text{f.dist.rt}(3.4016, 14, 14) = 0.0144$$

Since the probability of type I error is low enough, we reject the null hypothesis that the two variances are equal. Therefore, from Table 7.2, the following test statistics is used for testing equality of the mean prices for the two periods.

$$t = \frac{\left(\widehat{\mu_1} - \widehat{\mu_2}\right) - \left(\mu_1 - \mu_2\right)}{\sqrt{\frac{\widehat{\sigma_1^2}}{n_1} + \frac{\widehat{\sigma_2^2}}{n_2}}} = \frac{(32.32 - 31.27) - (0)}{\sqrt{\frac{0.10941}{14} + \frac{0.372182}{14}}} = \frac{1.05}{\sqrt{0.0344}}$$

$$= \frac{1.05}{0.185472} = 5.661232$$

Using the following Excel command we obtain the exact P value.

$$= \text{t.dist.rt}(5.6612, 28) = 0.000,002$$

Since the P value is low enough, we reject the null hypothesis that the average prices of Microsoft stock are the same for the periods of March 12–30 and April 2–21.

CHAPTER 8

An Introduction to Regression Analysis

Until this point, with the exception of covariance and correlation coefficient, the focus has been on a single variable. However, there are few, if any, economic phenomena that can be analyzed solely using its own information. Even in the simplest economic issues such as quantity demanded, there are at least two variables, a quantity and a price. Furthermore, many economic affairs are too complicated to be analyzed and explained fully by merely observing the matter by itself without any consideration to other economics, social, cultural, and political factors that usually affect most economic problems. For example, it does not suffice to analyze data on income in order to determine or forecast future incomes. Such a study does not provide a reasonable estimate of the current situation, let alone future forecasts. Let us explore, briefly, what other factors might affect income. First, we have to decide whether the orientation of the study is macro or microeconomics. At the microeconomics level the focus on income can be personal income or family income. For an individual, income is zero for many years. During these years the individual is growing up and attending school. In other words, he or she is acquiring human capital, which will affect earned income when the individual secures a job. Other factors include one's natural ability, talent, work ethic, exertion, years of experience, and seniority, to name a few. There are some other factors that, at least in theory, should not have an effect on one's income, but in reality they do, such as gender and race. At the macroeconomics level the determinants of income, which in this case should be referred to as the national income, are functions of the nation's productivity, its resources, population size, education levels, economic cycles, seasonal cycles, and other factors.

There are many powerful tools in statistical analysis that permit incorporating the factors that determine a phenomenon such as income. One such tool is regression analysis. The regression methodology acknowledges that most real life occurrences are subject to random error. Take, for example, the income of a person. It is easy to calculate the average income of the nation. Let us take a single person and compare his or her income to the average. Chances are that the income of the person is not going to be the same as the national average. One can argue that it would be unreasonable to expect the income of a person chosen at random to be the same as the average income of the nation because the person is likely to have a different level of education, years of experience, talent, ambition, health, and so forth than the average person. All of these do affect income. The important thing is that even if we account for all reasonable sources of differences between two people, there still will be a difference in income due to random factors beyond our control, recognition, or ability to measure them. The presence of difference between observations is nothing new, and we addressed that when we discussed the concept of individual error and error in general throughout this text. In the case of comparing a person to the average, most of the difference can be attributed to the differences in the influencing factors such as education, experience, and talent. In regression analysis, we try to account for these sources of influence and "explain" part of the error. Recall that a basic definition of error in statistics is "whatever that cannot be explained." So the deviation of one person's income from the average income is called individual error. In statistics it makes more sense to talk about averages because of the existence of random error. Averaging things removes the random error, which by definition has an expected value or an average equal to zero. In Chapter 2, we introduced variance, which gives a measure of error. In the same chapter we discussed standard deviation, which is the average error. In regression analysis we explain the part of the error that is caused by differences in the factors that affect the phenomenon of interest, in this case the income. After accounting for the role of all the influencing factors that determine income, there is a random component that remains unexplainable, which by definition becomes the new "error."[1] Briefly, the regression analysis is designed to minimize the squares of errors of observations from a hypothetical line that provides a relationship between a dependent variable, such as income, and an independent variable such as education. Note that errors are simply deviations of observations from the expected value. In descriptive statistics the expected value is simply the mean. In regression analysis, the regression line is the expected value.

We can extend the simple regression analysis from the case of one variable to as many variables as deemed necessary. As the number of explanatory variables increases, the regression model should be able to explain more of the deviations in the dependent variable, which in our example is the income. This statement is valid only if we have the correct determining factors, are also called independent variables and, all the appropriate independent variables are included without having irrelevant variables in the model. In the above example, the independent variables are education, years of experience, talent, ambition, and so forth. As mentioned earlier, there are factors that influence the dependent variable even though they should not, such as gender and race, and factors that influence income but cannot be controlled or anticipated by the model, such as a war, natural disaster, and so on. We include these variables in the models as **control variables**. Control variables such as war or natural disaster have good economic explanations. They are the variables that are assumed constant under the *ceteris paribus* assumption of economic theory.

The simple regression model consists of one dependent variable and one independent variable plus an error term.

$$\text{Income} = \beta_0 + \beta_1 \, \text{Education} + \varepsilon \qquad (8.1)$$

where, income is the dependent variable,

education is the independent variable,

β_0 is the intercept,

β_1 is the slope, and

ε is the error term.

This chapter is a brief introduction to a vast topic.[2] The independent variable is believed to be outside of the model and is not to be explained in any manner. Here we are not interested in why people obtain the level of education they do. Instead we are observing one's educational level and use it to explain his or her income. The dependent variable is endogenous to the model, which means the model is used to estimate the value of the dependent variable based on the level of income. In other words, the model determines the income, given a specific value of education. The Greek letters β_0 and β_1 are the parameters of the model. They are also called the intercept and the slope, respectively. The interpretation of β_1 is that for every unit change in education, income will change by the magnitude of β_1 and in the direction of its sign. The intercept β_0 provides an estimate of income when one has zero education. Finally, ε the error term, accounts for everything else that affects income, other than education, plus the random error inherent in real phenomena.

This simplistic model explains income with one variable. The hypothesized claim for the slope of the regression line, β_1, is that it is expected to be positive. This claim is based on theory and common sense. One expects higher income with more education, since education is a kind of investment called human capital. An educated person is more knowledgeable and hence, more productive, and thus deserves higher income per unit of time than someone with less education, other things equal. There are several advantages to using regression analysis. One of the more important ones is the fact that not only can we measure the contribution of the determinants of a dependent variable such as income, but we can also test to see if the determinants are actually significant. A typical inference about a regression model consists of two different tests. The one that tests the overall significance of the model is based on the F test. In this case, the amount of the variation in the dependent variable that is explained by the model is compared to the amount that still remains unexplained. The portion that is explained by the model is called **mean squared regression (MSR)**. Recall that the sum of squares of the portions not explained, divided by appropriate degrees of freedom is the same as variance, which in the jargon of regression analysis is called **mean squared error (MSE)**. In Chapter 4, we explained that the variance has a chi-squared distribution. The MSR also has a chi-squared distribution since it has similar distributional properties as a variance. Theorem 4.5 from Chapter 4 states that the ratio of two chi-squared distribution functions follows an F distribution. Therefore, we can use an F statistics to test the relative magnitude of the portion of the variation in the dependent variable that is explained by the model to the portion that is not. The null and alternative hypotheses for the model are:

$$H_0: \text{Model is not good} \qquad H_1: \text{Model is good}$$

The testing procedure is the same as before. If the p value is small enough, reject the null hypothesis; otherwise, fail to reject it. Once the above null hypothesis is rejected, then the individual slopes are tested for significance. The customary null hypothesis is that the slope of interest is zero. When a slope is zero it indicates that the corresponding variable does not have any explanatory power, and it does not contribute to the reduction of the variations in the error.

$$H_0: \beta_{Education} = 0 \qquad H_1: \beta_{Education} > 0$$

The appropriate test statistics for this hypothesis is a t statistics. Testing procedure is the same as usual. Reject the null hypothesis if the corresponding p value is low enough. All software designed to perform statistical analysis can perform regression analysis with a relatively easy set of commands or procedures, or both. In fact, many of the commercially available software are menu-driven, similar to a typical application software. Most have reasonably good help features that will show the necessary steps or commands. Even Microsoft Excel, a spreadsheet software, has a menu driven procedure to perform regression analysis, to provide test statistics for testing the model and slopes, and to provide estimates of slopes and the explanatory power of the model.[3]

Example 8.1

Let us test the hypothesis that education increases income. As pointed out earlier, there are numerous measures of income, from per capita personal income to the national income; the former represented a microeconomics aspect of income, while the latter is a macroeconomics perspective.[4] Care must be taken to analyze the data in light of its nature and not to imply or indicate more than the meaning of the outcome. The data is presented in Table 8.1.

Table 8.1. Data on Education and Income from 1970 to 2010 for the United States

Year	Total	Elementary		High school		College		Income
		Up to 4	5 to 8	<4	>=4	<4	>=4	
1975	116,897	4,912	20,633	18,237	42,353	14,518	16,244	1.33E+09
1976	118,848	4,601	19,912	18,204	43,157	15,477	17,496	1.47E+09
1977	120,870	4,509	19,567	18,318	43,602	16,247	18,627	1.63E+09
1978	123,019	4,445	19,309	18,175	44,381	17,379	19,332	1.83E+09
1979	125,295	4,324	18,504	17,579	45,915	18,393	20,579	2.05E+09
1980	130,409	4,390	18,426	18,086	47,934	19,379	22,193	2.29E+09
1981	132,899	4,358	17,868	18,041	49,915	20,042	22,674	2.57E+09
1982	135,526	4,119	17,232	18,006	51,426	20,692	24,050	2.76E+09
1983	138,020	4,119	16,714	17,681	52,060	21,531	25,915	2.94E+09
1984	140,794	3,884	16,258	17,433	54,073	22,281	26,862	3.26E+09
1985	143,524	3,873	16,020	17,553	54,866	23,405	27,808	3.48E+09
1986	146,606	3,894	15,672	17,484	56,338	24,729	28,489	3.68E+09
1987	149,144	3,640	15,301	17,417	57,669	25,479	29,637	3.91E+09
1988	151,635	3,714	14,550	17,847	58,940	25,799	30,787	4.22E+09
1989	154,155	3,861	14,061	17,719	59,336	26,614	32,565	4.54E+09
1990	156,538	3,833	13,758	17,461	60,119	28,075	33,291	4.83E+09
1991	158,694	3,803	13,046	17,379	61,272	29,170	34,026	5.01E+09
1992	160,827	3,449	11,989	17,672	57,860	35,520	34,337	5.34E+09
1993	162,826	3,380	11,747	17,067	57,589	37,451	35,590	5.56E+09
1994	164,512	3,156	11,359	16,925	56,515	40,014	36,544	5.87E+09
1995	166,438	3,074	10,873	16,566	56,450	41,249	38,226	6.19E+09
1996	168,323	3,027	10,595	17,102	56,559	41,372	39,668	6.58E+09
1997	170,581	2,840	10,472	17,211	57,586	41,774	40,697	6.99E+09
1998	172,211	2,834	9,948	16,776	58,174	42,506	41,973	7.52E+09
1999	173,754	2,742	9,655	15,674	57,935	43,176	43,803	7.91E+09
2000	175,230	2,742	9,438	15,674	58,086	44,445	44,845	8.55E+09
2001	180,389	2,810	9,518	16,279	58,272	46,281	47,228	8.88E+09
2002	182,142	2,902	9,668	16,378	58,456	46,042	48,696	9.05E+09
2003	185,183	2,915	9,361	16,323	59,292	46,910	50,383	9.37E+09
2004	186,876	2,858	8,888	15,999	59,811	47,571	51,749	9.93E+09
2005	189,367	2,983	8,935	16,099	60,893	48,076	52,381	1.05E+10
2006	191,884	2,951	8,791	16,154	60,898	49,371	53,720	1.13E+10
2007	194,318	2,830	8,462	16,451	61,490	49,243	55,842	1.19E+10
2008	196,305	2,599	8,226	15,516	61,183	50,994	57,787	1.25E+10
2009	198,285	2,785	8,043	15,587	61,626	51,670	58,574	1.19E+10
2010	199,928	2,615	7,836	15,260	62,456	51,920	59,840	1.24E+10

First, we regress income on the total number of people in the United States with education, regardless of the level of education.[5] See Table 8.2. The regression output is obtained from Excel. We will focus on the row named "Total," which refers to the name we used for the independent variable representing education. Remember that the data for education are represented in thousands of people. The coefficient for the independent variable is 127,095.6414. Therefore, for every 1,000 people who are educated, the income increases by $127,095. The other information in the output indicates that the model is a good model.

Next, let us regress the income on the number of people with four or more years of college (see Table 8.3).

The coefficient for the independent variable "4 or more years of college education" is $253,879. This indicates that for every 1,000 persons obtaining four or more years of college education, income increases by

Table 8.2. Regression of Income on Total Education from 1970 to 2010 in the United States

SUMMARY OUTPUT

Regression statistics	
Multiple R	0.977959617
R Square	0.956405013
Adjusted R Square	0.955287192
Standard Error	779350434.8
Observations	41

ANOVA

	df	SS	MS	F	Significance F
Regression	1	5.19679E+20	5.2E+20	855.5983	3.81799E–28
Residual	39	2.36881E+19	6.07E+17		
Total	40	5.43367E+20			

	Coefficients	Standard error	t stat	p-value
Intercept	–14108412049	680868741.5	–20.7212	1.18E–22
Total	127095.6414	4345.059321	29.25061	3.82E–28

Table 8.3. Regression of Income on Four or More Years of College Education from 1970 to 2010 in the United States

SUMMARY OUTPUT

Regression statistics	
Multiple R	0.9925175
R Square	0.98509099
Adjusted R Square	0.9847087
Standard Error	455762886
Observations	41

ANOVA

	df	SS	MS	F	Significance F
Regression	1	5.35266E+20	5.35E+20	2576.867	3.08304E–37
Residual	39	8.10107E+18	2.08E+17		
Total	40	5.43367E+20			

	Coefficients	Standard error	t stat	p-value
Intercept	–3120662505	183892483.1	–16.97	1.33E–19
>=4	253879.32	5001.28153	50.76285	3.08E–37

$253,879. This figure is twice the $127,095 we obtained for overall increase in education attainment. Therefore, as expected, more education results in higher income for the country.

What do you think would happen if we regressed income on the number of people with less than 4 years of education? The average number of years of education in the United States is much higher than 4 years of education. A person with such a low educational level will cause a reduction in the expected income of the country. Let us see if the regression analysis can demonstrate this point. The result of regressing income on up to 4 years of elementary education is shown in Table 8.4.

As anticipated, the coefficient of the independent variable is negative, indicating that for every 1,000 people who are over 25 years of age the income declines by $3,751,795. Other statistics in the table indicate

Table 8.4. Regression of Income on up to 4 Years of Elementary Education

SUMMARY OUTPUT

Regression statistics	
Multiple R	0.901856924
R Square	0.813345911
Adjusted R Square	0.808559909
Standard Error	1612624517
Observations	41

ANOVA

	df	SS	MS	F	Significance F
Regression	1	4.41946E+20	4.41946E+20	169.9427	8.5373E–16
Residual	39	1.01422E+20	2.60056E+18		
Total	40	5.43367E+20			

	Coefficients	Standard error	t stat	p-value
Intercept	19434322304	1099162811	17.68102242	3.2E–20
Up to 4	–3751794.554	287798.0556	–13.03620535	8.54E–16

that the model is a good model. It is important to caution the reader that these models are very simplistic, and there are more issues that have to be addressed. A comprehensive study of the impact on education is a huge undertaking, and this brief introduction is not sufficient to identify the true impact of education on income. One shortcoming of these examples is that they do not consider other factors that affect income, as discussed earlier. The simple regression analysis is easily extended to include all the variables that a researcher deems necessary. The main determining factor for including a variable in a regression model is the theory in the discipline in which the research is conducted. In our case, the governing theory belongs to the field of economics.

$$\text{Income} = \beta_0 + \beta_1 \text{ Education} + \beta_2 \text{ Experience} \\ + \beta_3 \text{ Race} + \beta_4 \text{ Gender} + \beta_5 \text{ Determination} + \varepsilon \tag{8.2}$$

The previous model is a typical model based on the variables we identified earlier as important. Note that the list is not exhaustive. One reason is that social variables are somewhat correlated. Education is not really independent of race or gender. Although there is no justifiable reason for education to be influenced by race or gender, the reality in the United States is that it is. Similarly, there is no reason to include race and gender as control variables in the model explaining the determinants of income. However, the fact is that in the current US society these variables do affect the level of income, other things equal. The second reason for limiting the number of variables is that, usually few important variables are sufficient to provide reasonable estimates or forecasts of the dependent variable. Generally, if two models are performing about the same, the one with fewer variables is preferred. One variable merits additional comments. The variable is "determination." There is no doubt that the amount of effort that a person puts into his or her job does affect the resulting income. Thus, the hypothesized value of β_5 is positive. However, there is no acceptable way of measuring one's resolve or how much effort one puts into his or her job. It is fairly easy to identify those that slack off or those that exert themselves, but neither can be measured. More importantly, any arbitrary ranking or measurement of "determination" is inaccurate and incomplete in the sense that it cannot be compared because it is a not a cardinal measure. Frequently, we face this problem in economics. For example, there is no cardinal measure of utility, which is a very important economic concept. The discussion of how we deal with the inability to measure utility with cardinal measures is beyond the scope of this text. In the case of variables such as "determination" in regression model, we have two alternatives. The first one is to accept that it is not a measurable phenomenon and not worry about including it in the model. The consequence is that the error term is enlarged, and there will be more of the variation in the dependent variable that cannot be explained as compared to the case if we could measure "determination" and use it in the model. This exclusion has serious consequences and is usually covered under **misspecification** of the model. The second method is to use a proxy variable that could represent the desired variable, albeit, not precisely or accurately. Can you think of a good proxy for "determination"?

A typical way of writing a model with unknown number of variables is of the form:

$$Y = \beta_0 + \beta_1 X_1 + \beta_2 X_2 + \cdots + \beta_K X_K + \varepsilon \qquad (8.3)$$

Each beta represents the contribution of the corresponding factor to an explanation of the dependent variable, keeping all the other factors constant.

Regression analysis is a powerful and useful tool used in many areas of science but has a special place in economics. As one might expect, there are many issues that pertain to economic reality that need not be applicable to other areas of science. We have already seen two such cases. One is the fact that the independent variables are somewhat related to each other in economics. This is due to the fact that many, if not all economic factors are subject to the economics and social realities of the same country. The same applies to the individual firms and people in a country. In many other fields, it is much easier to ensure that exogenous variables are independent from each other, which is a requirement of regression analysis.[6] The second issue is the role of factors that are social in nature and reflect the social/cultural structure of a country. For example, the fact is that race and gender influence one's income. There is no theoretical reason for such a role, except racism and chauvinism. Consequently, a special branch of science has been created called **econometrics**.

CHAPTER 9

Conclusion

This text is a brief introduction to statistics. The main focus has been on the application, comprehension, interpretation, and a sense of appreciation for statistics. The hope is that the reader has become interested in statistics and will pursue the topic further. In fact, the main reason for including the regression chapter, Chapter 8, was to show additional possibilities that go beyond a single-variable analysis. It demonstrates that we can explore the influence of one or more variables on a variable of interest. Within the subject of regression, one can explore theoretical and empirical aspects of cross section and time series data. Regression analysis has been augmented to utilize data that are qualitative in nature. The qualitative data can be used as dependent variables or independent variables. Many economic decisions can be represented as qualitative dependent variables, for example, the decision to buy a good or not to buy it, obtain a college degree, take a vacation (i.e. consume leisure), or to save, to name a few. Qualitative variables can also be independent variables, such as race, gender, political persuasion, and nationality.

The domain of statistics is vast and covers numerous specialized fields such as econometrics, biostatistics, sampling, and actuary to name a few. However, there is not a field that does not utilize statistical analysis; from agriculture to zoology.

This text groups related topics and focuses on the interrelationship of different topics. The best way to see this is to refer to Table 1.1 in Chapter 1. The table divides descriptive statistics into two major categories of qualitative variables and quantitative variables. The scope of methods for quantitative variables is much broader than those for the qualitative variables because the methods used for qualitative variables are also applicable for the quantitative variable, but the reverse is not true necessarily. Within each category the analytical methods are broken down to tabular methods and graphical methods. Recall that these are all descriptive methods and their purpose is to provide insight to the nature of data and to condense the massive amount of information into as few parameters as possible. Although graphical and tabular methods are very helpful in providing a visual description of data, the analytical power of statistics is more evident in the numerical methods that apply to quantitative variables. Within the last category, it is customary to distinguish among three different classifications: measures of central tendency, measures of dispersion, and measures of association. Each of these measures provides different refinements to analytical power and allows researchers to differentiate among different types of data where certain aspects might be similar while the nature of data are very different, for example, as in the case of two populations with the same means but different variances. The knowledge about parameters provides an insight into the nature of data. Massive databases are like chaos of numbers. In spite of the fact that the human brain is extremely good at finding order in events when the order is not easy to detect, the data is too large, or the relationships are too complex, it needs statistics to comprehend what is going on. A good example to clarify the above point is the saying "to miss the forest for the trees." Statistics provides a way of summarizing the evidence. The advantage of statistics is that it provides numerous descriptive and analytical tools that were not available prior to the discovery of statistics. Now it is possible to determine, with an appropriate level of probability, the outcome of a certain phenomenon or how to explain one or more variables using one or more other variables.

In Chapter 3, we put the few descriptive tools that were introduced in Chapter 2 into use by showing the applications of Z score and coefficient of determination. The chapter also provided additional tools to deepen the knowledge about life and to improve the analytical power of statistics. The concept of error is one of the major contributions of statistics to science. This notion allows us to divide variations in a phenomenon, which is ever-present in all real life situations, into two components: one that can be explained by statistical analysis and one that cannot be explained. One object of statistical analysis is to reduce the magnitude of the part that is unexplained. For example, the mean of a data explains part of the variation in it and leaves a part unexplained. In Chapter 8, we saw a glimpse of a regression analysis where part of the previously "unexplainable" error is explained by appropriate independent variables that are identified by economic theories or theories of other disciplines. This is just the beginning. There are numerous modifications to the simple regression analysis that allows us to reduce the unexplained portion by use of theory, assumptions, facts, prior information, and mathematical manipulations.

One mathematical manipulation is the discovery of different kinds of distribution functions. These mathematical relationships have certain known properties that are used to conduct statistical inference. They are also used to compare actual data to them and to apply the properties of these distribution functions to the actual data. The most important of such distribution functions is the normal distribution function. Although many natural events resemble the normal distribution function, many do not. Nevertheless, the use of theorems such as the Chebyshev's theorem and the Central Limit Theorem allows us to use the properties of the normal distribution in dealing with some of the statistics obtained from real data that either have a complicated distribution function or do not even have a known distribution function. For example, the distribution function of the quantity demanded of a good is usually unknown. However, we can use the theories mentioned previously to address the average quantity demanded. The link between the above theorems and statistics is the main subject of sampling distribution of sample statistics. We devoted Chapter 5 to this topic exclusively. The next step after identifying the distributional properties of the sample statistics is to use them to make inferences about population parameters. Population parameters determine the population and the underlying laws that govern them. The knowledge of parameters is similar to the knowledge about the phenomenon of interest, but in a manageable way.

The content of this text is a small portion of basic statistics. The next step for most economists is to learn regression analysis. The first step would be to learn simple and multiple regression for cross section data followed by the use of the same techniques modified to handle time series data. Almost all economic programs require at least one course in econometrics, which is the application of linear models such as regression analysis to economic issues. More serious students that pursue graduate work in economics are required to learn and sometimes prove the applicable theorems used in econometrics; however, a purely pragmatic approach of learning the methods is utilized by many programs. The next logical step is to combine the cross section and time series data, which since 1990 has become a distinct area commonly known as **panel data analysis.** In panel data analysis the problems that cause difficulty in the regressions using cross section or time series data are utilized to provide a better analysis. For example, the existence of correlation among units over time and the presence of correlations among independent variables are incorporated into the analysis rather than excluded or avoided. Probably the best example of this point is the analysis based on **seemingly unrelated data.** In this methodology, the fact that similar firms are subject to similar economic conditions and thus respond in similar manners in certain areas is the foundation of the methodology. Another recent development is **spatial econometrics** where the space related information is incorporated in the form of weight assigned to economic events. For example, it is reasonable to expect "neighboring" countries to act more similar than distant counties. There are numerous ways of defining neighbors, such as distance, existence of border, and so forth.

Finally, the hope is that the present text has been able to answer some of the questions readers had and also to spark an interest in this fascinating subject.

Glossary

Bar graph is a graphical representation of the frequency distribution or relative frequency distribution when dealing with qualitative data.

Binomial distribution function is a probability distribution representing a dichotomous binary variable.

Box plot is a visual representation of several basic descriptive statistics in a concise manner.

Categorical variable is another name for a qualitative variable.

Center of gravity of the data is the same as the expected value, or mean.

Central Limit Theorem states that in repeated random samples from a population, the sample mean will have a distribution function approximated by normal distribution, the expected value of the sample mean is equal to the true value of the population mean, and the variance of the sample mean is equal to population variance divided by the sample size.

Ceteris paribus is Latin for "other things being equal."

Chi-square represents the distribution function of a variance.

Claim is a testable hypothesis.

Coefficient of variation is the ratio of the standard deviation to the mean.

Confidence interval provides a probabilistic estimate of a population parameter with a desired level of confidence.

Consistent means the sample variance becomes smaller as sample size increases.

Continuous dichotomous variables exist when one can place an order on the type of data.

Continuous variable random is a variable that can assume any real value. It represents all the values over a range.

Correction factor with the variance is used when the sample size is small or the sample is more than 5% of the population.

Cross sectional analysis is a study of a snapshot of regions at a given time.

Cumulative frequencies consist of sum of frequencies up to the value or class of interest.

Deductive statistics start from general information to make inferences about specifics.

Degree of freedom is the number of elements that can be chosen freely in a sample.

Dependent variable is the variable of interest that is explained by statistical analysis. Other names such as endogenous variable, *Y*-variable, response variable, or even output are often used as well.

Descriptive statistics provide a descriptive, instead of analytic view, of variables.

Dichotomous variables, also called dummy variables in econometrics, exist when there are only two nominal types of data.

Discrete dichotomous variable is a dichotomous variable that can take integer values.

Discrete random variables consist of integers only.

Dot plot represents frequencies as stacked dots. It is useful when only one set of data is under consideration.

Dummy variable is a qualitative variable used as an independent variable.

Econometrics is the application of statistics to economics.

Efficient refers to the estimator with the smallest variance compared to the other estimator(s).

Error is the difference between an observed value and its expected value. Error is the portion of variation that cannot be explained.

Errors in measurement refer to incorrectly measuring or recording the values of dependent or independent variables.

Expected value is the theoretical value of parameter. It is the same as the arithmetic mean.

Experimental design is a type of statistics where the experiment is controlled for different variables to ensure desired levels of confidence for the estimates of the variable.

F statistics is used to test complex hypothesis. It consists of the ratios of two variance measures.

Frequency distribution shows the frequency of occurrence for non-overlapping classes.

Grouped data are summarized or organized to provide a better and more compact picture of reality.

Harmonic mean is the average of rates. It is the reciprocal of the arithmetic mean of the reciprocal of the values.

Histogram is a graphical representation of the frequency distribution or relative frequency distribution when dealing with quantitative data.

Independent variable is a variable that is used to explain the response or dependent variable. Other names such as exogenous variable, X-variable, regressor, input, factor, or predictor variable are also used.

Individual error is the difference between an observed value and its expected value.

Inductive statistics observes specifics to make inference about the general population.

Inferential statistics is the methodology that allows making decision based on the outcome of a statistics from a sample.

An **interval scale** includes relative distances of any two sequential values, such as a Fahrenheit scale.

Kurtosis is a measure of pointedness or flatness of a symmetric distribution.

A **Likert scale** is a kind of ordinal scale, where the subjects provide the ranking of each variable.

The **lower hinge** is the 25th percentile of a box plot.

Mean is the arithmetic average. It represents the center of gravity of data.

Mean absolute error (MAE) is the average of the absolute values of individual errors.

Mean squared error is the same as variance.

Measurement scales are types of variables.

Measures of association determine the association between two variables or the degree of association between two variables. They consist of covariance and correlation coefficient.

Measures of central tendency provide concise meaningful summaries of central properties of a population.

Measures of dispersion reflect how data are scattered. The most important dispersion measures are variance and standard deviation.

Median is a value that divides observations into two equal groups. It is the midpoint among a group of numbers ranked in order.

Mode is the most frequent value of a population.

Nominal or **categorical** data are the "count" of the number of times an event occurs.

Normal distribution is a very common distribution function that reflects many randomly occurring events in life.

Null hypothesis reflects the status quo or how things have been or are currently.

Observed significant level is another name for the p value, which is the probability of seeing what you saw.

Ogive is a graph for cumulative frequencies.

Ordinal scale indicates that data is ordered in some way but the numbering has no value.

***P* value** represents the probability of type I error for inference about a coefficient.

A **parameter** is a characteristic of a population that is of interest; it is constant and usually unknown.

A **percentile** is the demarcation value below which the stated percentage of the population or sample lie.

A **pie chart** is a graphical presentation of frequency distribution and relative frequency.

Point estimate is statistics that consists of a single value, such as mean or variance.

Probability is the likelihood that something will happen, expressed in the form of a ratio or a percentage.

Probability distribution determines the probability of the outcomes of a random variable.

Probability distribution for a continuous random variable is called a probability density function.

Probability distribution for a discrete random variable is called a discrete probability distribution and is represented as $f(x)$.

Qualitative variables are non-numeric and represent a label for a category of similar items.

Quantitative variables are numerical and countable values.

Quartiles divide the population into four equal portions, each equal to 25% of the population.

Random variables are selected in a random fashion and by chance.

A **ratio scale** provides meaningful use of the ratio of measurements.

Real numbers consist of all rational and irrational numbers.

Relative frequency shows the percentage of each class to the total population or sample.

Relative variability is the comparison of variability using coefficient of variation.

Reliability of a sample mean ($\hat{\mu}$) is equal to the probability that the deviation of the sample mean, from the population mean, is within the tolerable level of error (E).

Root mean squared error is the square root of the mean square error and is the same as the standard error.

Sample standard deviation is the average error of the sample. This is the standard deviation obtained from a sample and is not the same as standard error.

Sample statistics are random values obtained from a sample. They estimate the corresponding population parameters and are used to make inferences about them.

Sample variance is an estimate of the population variance. It is the sum of the squares of the deviations of values from the sample mean divided by the degrees of freedom.

Sampling is a subset of population that is collected in a variety of ways.

Sampling distribution of any statistics explains how the statistics differ from one sample to another.

Scatter plot is a graph customarily used in presenting data from a regression analysis model.

Simple hypothesis gives an exact value for the unknown parameter of the assumed distribution function.

Skewness refers to the extent that a distribution function deviates from symmetric distribution.

Standard deviation is the square root of variance and represents the average error of a population or sample.

Standard error is the standard deviation of the estimated sample statistics.

Standardization is the conversion of the value of an observation into its Z score.

A **statistic** is a numerical value calculated from a sample that is variable and known.

Statistical hypothesis is an assertion about distribution of one or more random variables.

Statistical inference is the process of drawing conclusions based on evidence obtained from a sample. All statistical inferences are probabilistic.

Stem-and-leaf is a graphical way of summarizing information and is a type of a descriptive statistics.

Stochastic means that a model is probabilistic in nature and would result in varying results reflecting the random nature of the model.

t **distribution** is a distribution function that is designed to handle statistics from small samples correctly.

A **testable hypothesis** is a claim about a relationship among two or more variables.

Time series analysis is the analysis of time series data.

Tolerable level of error is the amount of error that the researcher is willing to accept.

Tolerance level is a measure for detecting multicollinearity. It is the reciprocal of Variance Inflation Factor (VIF). A tolerance value less than 0.1 is an indicative of the presence of multicollinearity.

Total sum of square (TSS) represents the total variation in the dependent variable.

Trimmed mean is a modification of the mean, where outliers are discarded.

Type I error is rejecting the null hypothesis even though it is true.

Type II error is failure to reject a false hypothesis.

Type III error is rejecting a null hypothesis in favor of an alternative hypothesis with the wrong sign.

Typical refers to the average.

Unbiased refers to an estimate whose expected value is equal to the corresponding population parameter.

The **upper hinge** is the 75th percentile of a box plot.

Validity is the lack of measurement error.

Variance is the sum of the squares of the deviations of values from their mean, divided by population size. It is the average of the squared individual errors.

Weighted mean is similar to the mean except the weights for observation are not equal and represent their contribution to the total. Calculation of GPA is an example of weighted mean.

Z **score** is a statistics based on mean and standard deviation. It is used to standardize unrelated variables for the purpose of comparing them.

Notes

Chapter 1

1. Internal Revenue Service (2009).
2. Stevens (1946).
3. Tukey (1977).
4. Anderson et al. (2010).
5. Tukey (1977).

Chapter 3

1. Gosset (1908).
2. Gosset (1908).

Chapter 8

1. A more formal and detailed explanation of this process is available in Naghshpour (2012).
2. Interested readers should consult Naghshpour (2012) for more detailed discussion of the topic.
3. For more detail refer to Naghshpour (2012).
4. For the sake of this example, we use the national income that is obtained from http://www.bea.gov/histdata/Releases/Regional/2010/PI/state/preliminary _March-23-2011/SA1-3.csv. The data on education, which are in 1,000s, are obtained from http://www.census.gov/hhes/socdemo/education/data/cps /historical/index.html.
5. There is not enough space to discuss and explain all the numbers that are provided in Table 8.2, interested readers should consult Naghshpour (2012).
6. Naghshpour (2012).

References

Anderson, D. R., Sweeney, D. J., & Williams, T. A. (2011). *Statistics for business and economics*. South-Western College Publisher.

Anderson, D. R., Sweeney, D. J., & Williams, T. A. (2010). *Statistics for business and economics*. South-Western College Publisher.

Bureau of Economic Analysis, GDP and Personal Income: SA1-3 Personal Income Summary.

Bureau of Economic Analysis, National Income and Product Account Tables: Table 2.3.5-Personal Consumption Expenditures by Major Type of Product.

Gosset, W. S. (1908). Probable error of a correlation coefficient. *Biometrika 6*, 302–310.

Internal Revenue Service. (2009). SOI Tax Stats—Tax Stats at a Glance. Summary of Collections Before Refunds by Type of Return, FY 2009 [1]. http://www.irs.gov/taxstats/article/0,,id=102886,00.html

Naghshpour, S. (2012). *Regression for economics*. New York, NY: Business Expert Press.

Stevens, S. S. (1946). On the theory of scales of measurement. *Science 7*, 677–680.

Tukey, J. W. (1977). *Exploratory data analysis*. Reading, MA: Addison-Wesley.

Index

OTHER TITLES IN OUR ECONOMICS COLLECTION

Phil Romero, The University of Oregon and Jeffrey Edwards, North Carolina A&T State University, Collection Editors

- *Managerial Economics: Concepts and Principles* by Donald N. Stengel
- *Working With Economic Indicators: Interpretation and Sources* by Donald N. Stengel and Priscilla Chaffe-Stengel
- *Using Economic Data for Personal and Corporate Decision Making: What Have We Learned From California?* by Phillip J. Romero
- *Applying the Logic of the Five Forces Model to Your Products and Services. How Strong is Your Firm's Competitive Advantage?* by Daniel R. Marburger
- *Innovative Pricing Strategies to Increase Profits* by Daniel R. Marburger
- *Regression for Economics* by Shahdad Naghshpour

Announcing the Business Expert Press Digital Library

Concise E-books Business Students Need for Classroom and Research

This book can also be purchased in an e-book collection by your library as

- a one-time purchase,
- that is owned forever,
- allows for simultaneous readers,
- has no restrictions on printing, and
- can be downloaded as PDFs from within the library community.

Our digital library collections are a great solution to beat the rising cost of textbooks. e-books can be loaded into their course management systems or onto student's e-book readers.

The **Business Expert Press** digital libraries are very affordable, with no obligation to buy in future years. For more information, please visit **www.businessexpertpress.com/librarians**. To set up a trial in the United States, please contact **Adam Chesler** at *adam.chesler@businessexpertpress .com* for all other regions, contact **Nicole Lee** at *nicole.lee@igroupnet.com*.

CPSIA information can be obtained at www.ICGtesting.com
Printed in the USA
LVOW010518131212

311458LV00010B/364/P